Critical Discourse

Continuum Research Methods Series

Real World Research Series

Critical Discourse Analysis

Terry Locke

continuum
LONDON • NEW YORK

Continuum International Publishing Group
The Tower Building   15 East 26th Street
11 York Road   New York
London SE1 7NX   NY 10010

British Library Cataloguing-in-Publication Data
A catalogue record for this book is available from the British Library.

ISBN 0 8264 6486 6 (paperback)

Typeset by YHT Ltd, London
Printed and bound in Great Britain by Cromwell Press, Trowbridge Wiltshire

All my analyses are against the idea of universal necessities in human existence. They show the arbitrariness of institutions and show which space of freedom we can still enjoy and how many changes can still be made.

Michel Foucault (1982)

Contents

Acknowledgements

My first debt of gratitude is to those thinkers about language and its place in the world whose pioneering work made this book possible, in particular, Michel Foucault, Mikhail Bakhtin, Norman Fairclough, James Gee, Ruth Wodak and Teun van Dijk.

I would like to thank the *New Zealand Herald* for permission to publish the editorial that appears in Chapter 5. I am also grateful to the generosity of Oneroa Stewart who, in a number of emails, made it possible for me to contextualize this editorial. My thanks go to Lester Flockton and Professor Terry Crooks, for permission to use NEMP data for the transcript which is reproduced in Chapter 6. I would like to thank Michael Smither for permission to reproduce his painting 'Gifts' (Chapter 6) and the Collection of Museum of New Zealand: Te Papa Tangarewa, as owner of this work. My thanks also go to my colleague Graham Price who helped with the transcript used in Chapter 6.

1

A Close-up on Text

Critical discourse analysis in a nutshell

One of the founders of critical discourse analysis (CDA), Norman Fairclough, has described it as aiming

> to systematically explore often opaque relationships of causality and determination between (a) discursive practices, events and texts, and (b) wider social and cultural structures, relations and processes; to investigate how such practices, events and texts arise out of and are ideologically shaped by relations of power and struggles over power. (1995, p. 132)

Summed up in a number of bullet points, CDA:

- views a prevailing social order as historically situated and therefore relative, socially constructed and changeable.
- views a prevailing social order and social processes as constituted and sustained less by the will of individuals than by the pervasiveness of particular constructions or versions of reality – often referred to as discourses.
- views discourse as coloured by and productive of ideology (however 'ideology' is conceptualized).
- views power in society not so much as imposed on individual subjects as an inevitable *effect* of a way particular discursive configurations or arrangements

privilege the status and positions of some people over others.

- views human subjectivity as at least in part constructed or inscribed by discourse, and discourse as manifested in the various ways people *are* and *enact* the sorts of people they are.
- views reality as textually and intertextually mediated via verbal and non-verbal language systems, and texts as sites for both the inculcation and the contestation of discourses.
- views the systematic analysis and interpretation of texts as potentially revelatory of ways in which discourses consolidate power and colonize human subjects through often covert position calls. (For other precise accounts see Fairclough and Wodak 1997, Janks 1997, Wodak (1996, 2001).)

This book is about critical discourse analysis as a research method. However, CDA might be better described as a scholarly orientation with the potential to transform the modus operandi of a range of research methodologies. In respect of educational research, it has the potential to reveal the way power is diffused through the prevalence of various discourses throughout an education system, at both the micro-level of individual classrooms and the macro-level of large-scale reform. As in other settings, CDA has to be seen as a political intervention with its own socially transformative agenda.

A close-up

Some years ago, a billboard appeared near my home in Kingsland, Auckland. Against a white background were painted with brush-like, black strokes the words: 'Kelly

2

Browne's parents are away. PARTY at her place!!' (see Figure 1.1).

Figure 1.1 Kelly Browne Billboard

This is a text of just nine words and two sentences. A linguist might comment on the syntax by remarking that the first sentence is simple with a subject and one finite verb, and the second is either a noun phrase (a group of words built on the noun headword 'party') or a simple imperative sentence (where 'party' functions as an imperative verb telling people to party at Kelly's place). Such comments clearly utilize specialized linguistic vocabulary and will make sense to someone familiar with terms such as *simple sentence, subject, finite verb, noun phrase* and *imperative*. As a reader, you may find this linguistic information interesting, or you may be thinking, 'Do I need to know this?'!

There is, however, another way of approaching this text, which focuses more directly on the broad question, 'What does it mean?' To explore this question, I'd invite you to engage with a task I have used with a number of my students. To begin exploring the relationship between text and what I will be calling discourse, I show these students a reproduction of this billboard (see Figure 1.1). I point out that the text is made up of words, but that the writing has been done in a particular way (rather like graffiti). In doing so, I am introducing the idea that there are three types of signs: *icon* (where the sign resembles its object in some way, as in road signs); *index* (based on association or causality, e.g. graffiti signifying anti-social behaviour); and *symbol* (where the connection is convent-ional, e.g. a rose signifying love) (Hodge and Kress 1988: 21–3). I invite students to invent a 'story' that explains the connection between the first statement and the second.

As an educator of teachers and a researcher with an interest in language, what is interesting to me is the degree of consensus arrived at by the frequently diverse students involved. The consensus story might be told thus:

> Kelly Browne is in her late teens or early twenties and is still living at home with her parents. She is past the age where she feels the need to check out what she does with her parents. She likes to party, but can't imagine a party as being an occasion that includes parents. Parents, by defin-ition, are simply not party animals and tend to be some-what restrictive. Parties – real parties that is – are more about breaking out (and sometimes taboos and furniture). In general, then, a house without parents is an ideal locat-ion for a party.

Clearly, this consensus story has far more detail that the nine-word billboard. Despite the presence of dissenting voices, however (more on this below), it constitutes a coherent, widely subscribed to, interpretation of the billboard. Two questions immediately present themselves; 'Whence did this story originate?' and 'What is meant by the word *interpretation?*' These questions will turn out to be big ones and central to the subject of this book.

Whence stories?

In tackling the first question, we might begin by observing that the story cannot originate individually or collectively with the students. Their sense is of a story that is ready-made – something pre-existent and seemingly waiting for them to take up in the service of their meaning-making. We can further suggest that the story was not made up by the advertising agency that designed the billboard strategy. Advertising agencies, however innovative they may fancy themselves, in one respect make a virtue of being *un*-original. Ads are successful when they 'hit the spot' with the target audience; a successful ad appeals to a story or stories that its target audience habitually tells itself and is therefore sympathetic to. The makers of the Kelly Browne ad were appealing to a story (about young people, parties and parents) already current in the wider social context.

It appears that there are sense-making stories that can be viewed as circulating in society, that are not easily attributable to a particular originary source. The technical term for such a sense-making story is *discourse*. This term is variously defined (see Chapters 2 and 3). One definition regards a discourse as a coherent way of making sense of the world (or some aspect of it) as reflected in human sign systems (including verbal language). Norman Fairclough, one of the founders of CDA, draws on Michel Foucault in defining a discourse as 'a practice not just of representing the world, but of signifying the world, constituting and constructing the world in meaning' (1992a: 64). Questions of discourse will be explored in Chapters 2 and 3.

5

As we shall see, variations on the word *construct* (e.g. *construction, constructing*) are frequently found in CDA literature. (Indeed, they are a reminder that CDA is itself anchored in a discourse, a way of *constructing* the process of meaning-making in society.) In respect of the Kelly Browne ad, we might state that it constructs young people, parties and parents in particular ways:

- Young people prefer to socialize away from their parents.
- Parties are occasions for behaviour which parents may well disapprove of.
- Parents are party dampeners.

Listing constructions in this way highlights the *constructedness* of meaning. It also makes it easier to engage in acts of dissent – to take issue with these constructions and to *resist* the *storied meanings* any text is *positioning* one (another technical term) to subscribe to. When we accept a position that a text appears to be offering us or calling us to accept, we can be described as *interpellated* by it (a term coined by Althusser 1971). Certainly, my students were keen to emphasize the extent to which they *positioned themselves* in opposition to the discourse that was constructing young people, parties and parents in a particular way. Unsurprisingly, the dissenters were often mature students who were parents themselves and who objected to being *constructed* as non-partying animals.

There is another word in Fairclough's definition of discourse that bears reflecting upon because it raises another kind of issue; that is the word *constituting* as in the expression 'constituting the world in meaning'. Fairclough here is drawing on a key insight of Foucault's that 'discourse is in an active relation to reality, that language signifies reality in the sense of constructing meanings for it, rather than that discourse is in a passive relation to reality, with language merely referring to objects which are taken to be given in reality' (1992a: 41–2). The dictionary meaning of 'constitute' is 'to be; to go together to make'. Utilizing this definition, Fairclough's words might be rewritten: 'Discourse(s) make the world meaningful.' Or more strongly: 'Only in discourse is the world made meaningful.' There are clearly epistemological questions here, which I will simply raise. Questions such as: 'Is the world knowable outside of discourse?' and 'Can meaning-making take place outside of socially constructed signifying systems?'

Finally, there is another aspect of discourse that warrants comment. Fairclough, in his definition, also refers to discourse as a *practice*. While such a practice is reflected in human verbal and non-verbal signifying systems, it also embraces a range of human activities. In other words, a discourse implies ways of being and doing as well as ways of signifying. James Gee captures this aspect of discourse when he asserts that 'Discourses include much more than language':

> Discourses, then, are ways of behaving, interacting, valuing, thinking, believing, speaking, and often reading and writing that are accepted as instantiations of particular roles (or 'types of people') by specific *groups of people*, whether families of a certain sort, lawyers of a certain sort, bikers of a certain sort, business people of a certain sort, church members of a certain sort, African-Americans of a certain sort, women or men of a certain sort, and so on through a very long list. Discourses are ... 'ways of being in the world'; they are 'forms of life'. They are, thus, always and everywhere *social* and products of social histories. (1996: viii)

In the example of Kelly Browne, the notion of discourse (Gee tends to capitalize his use of the word in this sense) extends to the roles assumed and typical activities engaged in by people who are sympathetic to the constructions of young people, parents and party-going that the ad invites one to subscribe to.

Acts of interpretation

The second question draws attention to the act of interpretation that allowed these students to come up with a coherent interpretation of such a minimal text. What is interpretation and how did it happen? Interpretation arises from an act of reading or analysis which makes meaning of a text. Extending this definition, Fairclough argues that in respect of discourse analysis, interpretation focuses on three dimensions of discursive practice: (i) its manifestation in linguistic form (in the form of 'texts'); (ii) its instantiation of a social practice (political, ideological, and so on); and (iii) a third dimension which focuses on socially constructed processes of production, distribution and consumption which determine how texts are made, circulated and used.

These dimensions will be revisited in more detail in Chapters 4–6. However, at this juncture I would point out that:

- These three dimensions are not mutually exclusive.
- The first focuses on the text as a describable and patterned thing made out of language but extending to other related signifying systems such as the lettering style of the Kelly Browne ad (see Chapter 2).
- The second focuses on ways in which texts reflect larger patterns of social practice – ways of identifying, ways of thinking, ways of being in the world (see Chapter 3).
- The third focuses on the ways in which texts operate in the world, including how they are made, disseminated

and read. It also draws attention to the relationship *between* texts.

The latter point can also be illustrated in reference to the Kelly Browne billboard. I argued earlier that the ad's 'story' about young people, parties and parents was circulating before the ad makers decided to make use of it. The concept of *intertextuality* relates to ways in which texts are referenced to other texts by virtue of the stories (or discourses) embedded in them. Moreover, texts can refer forwards as well as backwards. The Kelly Browne billboard was specifically designed to link with other texts produced as part of what turned out to be an advertising campaign for an insurance company. But in ways that the billboard designers could not anticipate, the slogan was also taken up by others in 'intertextual acts'. (For example, a wag at a rugby game at Carisbrook, Dunedin, carried a placard with the words, 'Party at Tony Brown's place'. Tony Brown was the fly-half of the Otago rugby team playing that day.)

In the course of this chapter, and using a small text of nine words, we have engaged in an act of CDA. We can characterize this act as:

- *analytical* because we have conducted a detailed systematic examination of a particular object with a view to arriving at one or more underlying principles.
- *discourse* oriented in that this analysis has been concerned with language in use (one sense of the word 'discourse') and with the way in which patterns of meaning (as in stories that make the world meaningful) are socially constructed (the other sense of the word 'discourse').
- *critical* because a central outcome of the act of analysis is to enable consideration of the social effects of the meanings a reader is being positioned or called upon

9

to subscribe to in the act of reading, and the contestation of these meanings.

The remainder of the book shows how this act can be elaborated into a usable and potentially powerful research method. In the next chapter, I deal with language and its interplay with the term 'discourse'.

2

Language, Discourse and Context

Language is at the heart of critical discourse analysis. But how and why? One answer relates to what is sometimes termed the 'linguistic turn' in twentieth-century thought, which has changed language from being thought of as a medium for expressing meanings that pre-exist linguistic formulation to a system that constitutes meaningfulness in its own terms. With reference to the human sciences, Parker has noted a shift – what he calls a 'turn to discourse' – in the last 30 years 'from a notion of representation as a direct or mediated reflection of reality to a conceptual and methodological account of representation as a form of *signification*' (1999: 4–5) which actually shapes or constitutes the object denoted. Reality as preceding language and shaping it has become language preceding and shaping reality. Consequently, language has now come to occupy centre stage in scholarly investigation.

A recognition that meaning is – even in part – socially constructed via the mediation of language and other sign systems has a number of consequences. One is a view of meaning as historically and culturally situated as opposed to being eternal, absolute and essential. A second consequence, especially pertinent for researchers, is a need for reflexivity and provisionality. This requires researchers to acknowledge that particular research traditions construct the quest for and dissemination of new knowledge in ways that are culturally situated and mediated by particular forms of textual practice. As Fairclough has asserted, analysis cannot be separated from interpretation and analysts need to be 'sensitive to their own interpretative tendencies and social reasons for them' (1992a: 35). Yet again, we are being asked to confront the ways in which our language practices constrain the *how* and *what* of our claims to know.

This chapter briefly addresses some language issues and approaches to describing language. Questions of *what* and *how much* linguistic knowledge are required to undertake CDA are addressed in Chapter 4.

Literacy: individual cognition versus social construction

Traditionally literacy is defined as the ability to read and write texts – to decode writing (as a reader) and to code language in graphic form (as a writer). In this view, textual interpretation is psychological – something occurring in a reader's head. If you can decode and have the necessary background information, you can understand the meaning of a text (Gee 1996: 39). Meaning, then, is something that inheres in texts and corresponds with something 'out there' in the real world. Moreover, it tends to be unitary and sharable with other competent readers.

In using the word 'traditional', I do not want to be seen as denigrating cognitive approaches to language acquisition, the way human's process language, and how the mind works to make sense of the environment. Indeed, I have enormous respect for the contributions of cognitive neuroscience in this regard (for example, of Pinker (1994, 1997) and Damasio (1999)). However, the theories of language underpinning these approaches do not articulate readily with the concerns of CDA.

An alternative to this traditional view suggests that literacy be viewed not as a single thing but as a set of socially constructed practices that readers and makers of texts are apprenticed in as members of a particular social group. Not only do different types of text require different ways of reading, but the same text can also be read in different ways to generate different meanings. Textual meaning becomes multiple and therefore indeterminate. Literacy is now plural ('literacies') and characteristic of a social group's wider set of practices rather than something denoting the cognitive competence of a single individual. This sociocultural approach to literacy allows for the observation that some versions of 'literate' practice are discursively constructed as having higher status than others (Gee 1996, Pennycook 2001).

Discourse and text

Definitions of a number of terms used in this book are far from settled. A typical dictionary definition of 'discourse', for example (a formal speech or essay on a particular subject), is clearly remote from the sense(s) in which I have been using the term. Discourse analysis employs the term in two broad categories of use (Pennycook 2001, Paltridge 2000):

1   Discourse as an abstract noun denoting language in use as a social practice with particular emphasis on larger units such as paragraphs, utterances, whole texts or genres.
2   Discourse as a *countable* noun (one that permits pluralization) denoting a 'practice not just of representing the world, but of signifying the world,

constituting and constructing the world in meaning' (Fairclough 1992a: 64). This is Gee's (1996) 'Discourse' with a capital 'D'.

The first of these categories relates to the concerns of this chapter; the second to Chapter 3.

Writing from a social semiotic point of view, Hodge and Kress (1988) distinguish between message, text and discourse. The *message* is the smallest semiotic form, characterized by 'a source and a goal, a social context and purpose'. *Texts* and *discourses* are larger units. The writers distinguish between these in defining a 'text' as 'a structure of messages or message traces which has a socially ascribed unity' and a 'discourse' as 'the social process in which texts are embedded'. Texts, they emphasize, have their place in a social system of signs that is dynamic. 'So texts are both the material realization of systems of signs, and also the site where change continually takes place' (pp. 5–6).

Writing from a similar perspective, Halliday and Hasan (1985) define 'text' as 'language that is functional . . . that is, doing some job in some context, as opposed to isolated words or sentences'. Referring to a text as a 'semantic unit', they distinguish two perspectives whence it can be considered. On the one hand, a text is a *product*, produced in a particular time and place, a material artifact that can be described and analysed. On the other hand, it is a *process*, 'in the sense of a continuous process of semantic choice, a movement through the network of meaning potential, with each set of choices constituting the environment for a further set'. In its 'process' aspect, a text is necessarily linked to a society's linguistic system and can be thought of as an 'interactive event', a form of exchange that is dialogic in its nature (pp. 10–11). Such argumentation is designed to explain the way texts connect with their social context. Ideas such as interactivity and dialogue take us to a key theorist whose ideas about language and context have contributed greatly to the theoretical underpinnings of CDA – Mikhail Bakhtin.

Bakhtin: the utterance and speech genres

'The problem with speech genres', written in 1952–3, exemplifies Bakhtin's interest in theorizing about language in use (1986). His stated focus is the diversity of 'areas of human activity', from the reading of literary texts to informal conversation, and the role language plays in these. Each of these areas is characterized by its own set of conditions and the purposes at work for its participants. Central to his view is the claim that 'Language is realized in the form of individual concrete utterances (oral and written)' that participants make (p. 60).

For Bakhtin, the conditions that prevail in a particular area of human activity are reflected in the three constitutive features all utterances share (see below). These features are linked to the *whole* of the utterance and are determined by the specific nature of what he terms the 'particular sphere of communication'. For Bakhtin, different spheres of communication generate their own '*relatively stable types* of utterances'. These *types* he terms 'speech genres' (p. 60), writing: 'A particular function (scientific, technical, commentarial, business, everyday) and the particular conditions of speech communication specific for each sphere give rise to particular genres, that is, certain relatively stable thematic, compositional, and stylistic types of utterances' (p. 64).

In exploring the relationship between style and genre, it is clear that the individual has not been erased in Bakhtin's thinking by a concern for the social. For him, style is individual, but genres vary in the extent to which they are conducive to reflecting individual style. However,

15

the social is still a determining influence. Hence the oft-quoted sentence where Bakhtin connects language and society: 'Utterances and their types, that is, speech genres, are the drive belts from the history of society to the history of language' (p. 65).

The second major part of the essay focuses on the nature of the utterance itself. In a memorable passage, he introduces the idea of the 'organized chain of utterances', which underpins the concept of intertextuality (introduced in Chapter 1):

> Moreover, any speaker is himself a respondent to a greater or lesser degree. He is not, after all, the first speaker, the one who disturbs the eternal silence of the universe. And he presupposes not only the existence of the language system he is using, but also the existence of preceding utterances – his own and others' – with which his given utterance enters into one kind of relation or another (builds on them, polemicizes with them, or simply presumes that they are already known to the listener). Any utterance is a link in a very complexly organized chain of other utterances. (p. 69)

In a passage that anticipates Halliday and Hasan's use of the words 'interactivity' and 'dialogic', Bakhtin writes: 'The utterance is filled with *dialogic overtones*, and they must be taken into account in order to understand fully the style of the utterance. After all, our thought itself – philosophical, scientific, and artistic – is born and shaped in the process of interaction and struggle with others' thought, and this cannot but be reflected in the forms that verbally express our thought as well' (p. 92). Importantly, Bakhtin's dialogism is both retrospective and anticipative. The latter he terms *addressivity*, and refers to ways in which utterances are constructed to take account of possible future responses.

For Bakhtin, the boundaries of each concrete utterance

as a unit of linguistic communication are determined by a *change of speaking subjects,* that is, a change of speakers. This is the first of three constitutive features of the utterance. The second is what he calls its *finalization,* which has three aspects:

1   Semantic exhaustiveness of the theme.
2   The speaker's plan or speech will.
3   Typical compositional and generic forms of finalization.

The first of these we might roughly equate with *content,* the second with *purpose* and the third with *textual form* or *text type.* It is the last of these, which Bakhtin identifies as most important to his purpose, and which relates to the key notion of genre as employed in CDA. 'We speak only in definite speech genres, that is, all our utterances have definite and relatively typical *forms of construction of the whole.* Our repertoire of oral (and written) speech genres is rich' (p. 78).

Bakhtin's third constitutive feature is 'the relation of the utterance to the *speaker himself* (the author of the utterance) and to the *other* participants in speech communication' (p. 84). Here, Bakhtin distinguishes two aspects, which determine choice of linguistic means and speech genre:

1   'the referentially semantic assignments (plan) of the speech subject (or author)'.
2   'the *expressive* aspect, that is, the speaker's subjective emotional evaluation of the referentially semantic content of his utterance' (p. 84). As a case in point, Bakhtin notes how a dictionary, while it may indicate the stock of words that a culture has at its disposal, cannot account for the way words are used in

17

utterances, since this is always individual and contextual.

In conclusion, Bakhtin's concept of genre points to the
typical forms of construction of an utterance. It is social in
origin (in that it recalls past utterances and anticipates
future ones); yet there is a clear emphasis on individual
agency and creativity. While a description of a speech
genre may refer to such formal features as vocabulary,
syntax and structure, it is the social context that elicits
them and makes them meaningful.

Social context, genre and the 'new rhetoric'

The relationship of the lexicon (dictionary) to the social
context of the utterance can be thought of as exempli-
fying the way in which codified sign systems in general
(verbal, visual, behavioural) are rendered meaningful
only in relationship to the social structures which constitute them. In terms of the development of CDA, the
most important theorist of the text/context relationship
has been M. A. K. Halliday, who developed systemic
functional grammar (see Chapter 4) out of a social-
semiotic perspective on language.

In the 1980s, Halliday developed a framework for
describing what he termed the *context of situation*, the
social context of a text which allowed for meaning to be
exchanged.

1   The *field of discourse* is the general sense of what a
     text is about and refers to 'what is happening, to the
     nature of the social action that is taking place'. This
     aspect is comparable to Bakhtin's sphere of com-
     munication.
2   The *tenor of discourse* is concerned with the partici-

pants, their relationship, their roles and relative status.

3   The *mode of discourse* focuses on what the language is being ask to do – its function – the way it is organized, the medium (print, spoken, and so on) and also 'the rhetorical mode, what is being achieved by the text in terms of such categories as persuasive, expository, didactic, and the like' (Halliday and Hasan 1985: 12).

Halliday's context of situation denoted only the immediate environment for a textual event. He introduced the term *context of culture* for the broader institutional and cultural environment within which the context of situation is embedded.

Halliday's colleague, Ruqaiya Hasan, in addressing questions of textual structure, used the term *contextual configuration* to denote the variable interrelationship between field, tenor and mode. For her, identification of a text's contextual configuration can make sense of a text's structure. It also relates to genre, which, like Bakhtin, she regards as a socialized language practice. So what is genre? Hasan states quite simply that a genre is the 'verbal expression' of a contextual configuration. Specific genres (for example, expository essays, résumés, reports, various oral genres, and so on) are characterized by what Hasan calls their *generic structure potential* – their 'obligatory' elements (those that *must* occur); their 'optional' elements (those that *can* occur), the possible placement for elements and their potential for recurrence ('iteration'). What we have here is a potential for structural variability in the same genre but within limits (ibid.: 55–6, 64, 108).

We will be returning to Halliday and Hasan in Chapter 4. In the meantime, Halliday's use of the expression 'rhetorical mode' connects with another approach to thinking about the relationship of text to context: the 'new rhetoric' (Andrews 1992). At its most simple, rhetoric (in its refurbished sense) is the art of making language work. Function is the work that language performs at a particular instance in a text. A rhetorical approach to text can be summed up in the following points:

- People construct texts to achieve a desired result with a particular audience.
- Textual form follows function.
- Texts are generated by contexts.
- Texts assume a social complicity between maker and reader.
- The expectations of participants in such acts of complicity become formalized in the conventions of genre.
- These conventions relate to such language features as layout, structure, punctuation, syntax and diction.

Like other terms in this book, 'genre' signifies different things in different approaches to the text/context relationship. Bakhtin uses it in two senses, for both the complex of factors that make up the utterance as he defines it and the 'form of construction' of the utterance as textual product. Hasan's focus is clearly on the text as verbal expression. Kress, in his early work, echoes Hasan in defining genres as 'typical forms of text which link kinds of producer, consumer, topic, medium, manner and occasion' (Hodge and Kress 1988: 7).

Writers in the new rhetorical tradition incline to definitions of genre focusing on similarities in the context of situation (to use Halliday's term) rather than in the text as artefact. Freedman and Medway, for instance, define genres as 'typical ways of engaging rhetorically with recurring situations' (1994: 2). By the early 1990s, Kress was viewing genre similarly, defining it as 'the conventionalised aspect of the interaction' while asserting that the text in its social and cultural context was the necessary starting point for any worthwhile consideration of the forms, uses and functions of language (Kress 1993: 24). Like Freedman and Medway, he argues that it is the stability and repeatability of a social situation that leads to stability and conventionality in textual forms. These differing approaches to genre need not be seen as problematic to CDA. Indeed, they might be seen as the complementary process/product sides of a reasonably coherent approach to textual analysis.

The following headings are useful for describing a genre:

1   Context of culture
2   Context of situation
3   Function/purpose
4   Typical content
5   Features:
    • layout
    • diction
    • punctuation
    • syntax
    • structure.

Box 2.1 is an example of a description of a magazine feature article.

Box 2.1   Describing a magazine feature article

1	**Context of culture:** magazines have a prominent and pervasive place in Western culture. Feature articles are the 'staple' genre to be found in most magazines.
2	**Context of situation:** feature articles tend to be topical, dealing with issues, people and events of interest to a magazine's readers.

3   **Function/purpose:** feature articles fulfil a range of functions (informing, investigating, describing, arguing for a position). To help sell magazines, they also need to be stylish, engrossing, amusing or entertaining.

4   **Typical content:** feature articles typically background a topical issue, such as the profile of a prominent person. Depending on the magazine, there may be an emphasis on researched information or reliance on hearsay and gossip.

5   **Features:**
   - *layout:* bold headlines, subheadings and sections, photographs and captions, columns, usually two fonts and text justification.
   - *diction:* the degree of formality is affected by the pitch (i.e. the audience aimed at). Depending on pitch and content, diction may be more or less figurative, embellished, plain or colloquial.
   - *punctuation:* in general, punctuation follows formal conventions. The presence of direct speech will necessitate speech markers (inverted commas, usually).
   - *syntax:* again, this will be affected by the level of formality. In general, however, syntax tends to follow formal, correct usage with plenty of instances of subordination and coordination and cohesive devices.
   - *structure:* here is a typical structure:
     i   Begins with an initial focus which sets the scene.
     ii   Moves to the general topic which is being written about.
     iii   Topic is dealt with at length, often with a variety of points of view drawn upon.
     iv   Article is rounded of by revisiting the initial focus.

The categorization of features used in Box 2.1 is affected by the use of a print text example. As early as

1988, Hodge and Kress were insisting that in contemporary society, meaning resides strongly and pervasively in systems other than the verbal, especially the visual (p. vii). Hypertext, the medium of the Internet, is an important, multimodal signifying system. There are, I would argue, two ways in which a print genre might be 'refeatured' under pressure from the hypertextual medium. The first of these is in terms of feature categories. The five categories listed in terms of a print genre above start to break down when used, for example, to describe a print text with certain graphic elements. For example, in respect of a magazine display advertisement, composition is a key category of feature. Should one make this a sixth feature? Or combine it with layout under the category of 'Design'?

What categories might serve for categorizing the features of a hypertext? I would suggest:

- architecture (for three-dimensional aspects of design, for example, patterns of intra-page and extra-page linkage)
- composition (for two-dimension aspects of design, for example, the nature of the template and the relationship of word-based and graphic-based elements within a page)
- verbal diction and syntax (for aspects of diction and syntax within word-based elements on a site)
- graphic diction and syntax (for aspects of diction and syntax within graphic-based elements on a site)
- aural elements: voiced word language, sound effects and music
- thematic organization and cohesion (for ways in which elements on a page and between pages are organized thematically).

I am raising these issues here, rather than in Chapter 4,

because changes in information and communications technology, especially under pressure from digitalization, have been profoundly affecting textual practice which, we need to keep reminding ourselves, is not just socially but also technologically mediated. One of the challenges facing CDA is to expand its theoretical repertoire for describing texts to include the new and hybrid text-types spawned by the digital revolution.

3

The Critical Turn: Making Discourse Analysis Critical

The word 'critical' is a ubiquitous epithet attached to a variety of nouns: 'critical literacy', 'critical theory', 'critical approaches', 'critical applied linguistics', and so on. Like other terms used in this book – 'genre' for example – it means different things to different people. Different discourses construct 'critical' and 'critique' in various ways. Kincheloe and McLaren (1994), in an overview of critical theory and qualitative research, describe as 'risky' attempts at identifying an underlying commonality among 'criticalists'. Nevertheless, they suggest a critical orientation assumes:

- that all thought is fundamentally mediated by power relations that are social and historically situated
- that facts can never be isolated from the domain of values or removed from some form of ideological inscription
- that the relationship between concept and object and between signifier and signified is never stable or fixed and is often mediated by the social relations of capitalist production and consumption
- that language is central to the formation of subjectivity (conscious and unconscious unawareness)
- that certain groups in any society are privileged over others and, although the reasons for this privileging may vary widely, the oppression that characterizes contemporary societies is most forcefully reproduced when

> subordinates accept their social status as natural, neces-
> sary, or inevitable
> - that oppression has many faces and that focusing on only
>   one at the expense of others (e.g. class oppression versus
>   racism) often elides the interconnections among them
> - that mainstream research practices are generally,
>   although most often unwittingly, implicated in the
>   reproduction of systems of class, race, and gender
>   oppression. (pp. 139–40)

I cite the above list, not so much to endorse it as to communicate the discursive 'flavour' of the tradition that has constructed it.

Theorists and practitioners of CDA themselves endow the term with different shades of meaning. This is not surprising, since criticalist traditions in general, and CDA specifically, draw on distinct schools of social inquiry: the neo-Marxism of the Frankfurt school, Foucaultian archaeology, poststructuralist deconstruction and post-modernism (see Denzin and Lincoln, 1994: 140, van Dijk 1993: 251). Acknowledging these differences, Wodak writes that 'Basically, "critical" is to be understood as having distance to the data, embedding the data in the social, taking a political stance explicitly, and a focus on self-reflection as scholars doing research' (2001: 9).

In this chapter, I discuss the 'critical' under three headings: critique as revelation, critical practice as self-reflexive and critical practice as socially transformative. Rather than offering these headings as a prescription, I suggest that they be viewed as widespread tendencies. Indeed, there are tensions and even contradictions between ways in which the 'critical' can be viewed and lived.

Critique as revelation

In normal parlance, the word 'critical' denotes the habit of evaluating an object or situation in accordance with a system of rules, principles and values. I want to start with the work of Foucault, who located the 'critical' in the systematic, analytical endeavour to reveal the nature of systems of rules, principles and values as historically situated bases for critique. He called this analysis *archaeology* and its product a *genealogy*; his key term was *discourse.*

Foucault's essay 'Politics and the study of discourse' first appeared in the French journal *Esprit* in 1968. Written two years after the publication of *The Order of Things: An Archaeology of the Human Sciences,* this brief work afforded Foucault the opportunity of both defining his project and defending it against the charge that his approach to cultural history militates against political radicalism. At this point in his career, Foucault summed up his project as follows:

> To determine, in its diverse dimensions, what the mode of existence of discourses and particularly of scientific discourses (their rules of formation, with their conditions, their dependencies, their transformations) must have been in Europe, since the seventeenth century, in order that the knowledge which is ours today could come to exist, and, more particularly, that knowledge which has taken as its domain this curious object which is man. (1991: 70)

His project, then, was an attempt at mapping the origin and development of ways of thinking which shape modern attempts to constitute human beings as objects of scientific inquiry.

Early in his essay, Foucault stresses that he is a 'pluralist' and sets out a set of criteria for *individualizing* discourses (e.g. medicine, psychiatry, grammar), which are plural, relative and dynamic 'entities'. (There is a distinct echo of Bakhtin when he notes how discourses such as sociology and psychology undergo constant changes as new utterances – énoncés – are added to them.) These criteria are:

1   Criteria of *formation*. For Foucault, what *individualizes* a discourse is 'the existence of a set of rules of formation' for *all* its objects, operations, concepts and theoretical options. 'There is an individualized discursive formation whenever it is possible to define such a set of rules' (p. 54). One archaeological aim, then, is to reveal the sets of rules, which allow for a discourse to construct its field (objects, operations, concepts, theoretical options) in particular ways and not others.

2   Criteria of *transformation* or of *threshold*. This criteria is concerned with discursive change. 'I shall say natural history or psychopathology are units of discourse, if I can define the set of conditions which must have been jointly fulfilled at the precise moment of time, for it to have been possible for its objects, operations, concepts and theoretical options to have been formed; if I can define what internal modifications it was capable of; finally if I can define at what threshold of transformation new rules of formation came into effect' (p. 54).

3   Criteria of *correlation*. These criteria are concerned with what makes a discursive formation (e.g. clinical medicine) 'autonomous' and, for Foucault, involve the ability to define it in relation to other discourses (e.g. biology, chemistry) and to its non-discursive context ('institutions, social relations, economic and political conjuncture') (p. 54).

These criteria collectively allow Foucaultian analysis to

reveal what he terms 'the *episteme* of a period' – not some totalizing grand theory of the sum of its knowledge – 'but the divergence, the distances, the oppositions, the differences, the relations of its various scientific discourses' (p. 55). What such analysis opens up is a *space* characterized by an unstable and complex interplay of discursive relationships.

Later, Foucault details his interest in what makes certain statements in a field possible – 'the law of *existence* of statements, that which rendered them possible – them and none other in their place: the conditions of their singular emergence; their correlation with other previous or simultaneous events, discursive or otherwise' (p. 59). The emphasis is not on the *sayer* (here Foucault diverges from Bakhtin) but on the *said*. Hence Foucault's avowed disinterest in the consciousness and intentionality of the speaking subject or individual creative genius. His archaeological method aims at the description of an *archive*, by which he means 'the set of rules which at a given period for a given society define':

1   'The limits and forms of the *sayable*. This is concerned with what can be said within a particular 'domain of discourse' and the form this speaking might take. (This touches on the question of 'genre', though Foucault does not use the word here.)

2   'The limits and forms of *conservation*'. This is concerned with the ways in which utterances emerge, persist, disappear and circulate.

3   'The limits and forms of *memory* as it appears in different discursive formations'. This concerns the extent to which certain utterances are subscribed to and viewed as valid at a particular time.

4   'The limits and forms of *reactivation*'. This is concerned with ways in which older or alien discourses

are 'retained', 'valued', 'imported' and 'reconstituted'.

5   'The limits and forms of *appropriation*'. This is concerned with *who* has access to *what* discourses. It includes questions such as 'How is the relationship institutionalised between the discourse, speakers and its destined audience?' and 'How is struggle for control of discourses conducted between classes, nations, linguistic, cultural or ethnic collectivities?' This last focus for definition is relevant to the third critical tendency I discuss later in this chapter (pp. 59–60).

What does 'critical' mean in the context of Foucault's archaeological method? In this essay, he views his approach as critical because it poses four challenges to traditional approaches to the history of thought.

1   The first establishes limits to the 'realm of discourse'. Foucault sees himself as issuing challenges:
    a   To the assumption that discursive meaning-making has 'no assignable frontier'.
    b   To the assumption of a meaning-making subject 'which constitutes meanings and then transcribes them into discourse' (replaced by the subject as always discursively constituted).
    c   To the assumption of 'indefinitely receding origin', which I might paraphrase as discursive continuity in time, which Foucault replaces with the assignation of 'thresholds and conditions of birth and disappearance' (pp. 61–2).
2   The second eliminates certain binary oppositions, for example, 'traditions and invention', old and new, 'the dead and the living', 'the closed and the open' and 'the static and the dynamic' (p. 62).
3   The third – and most important – is to end what

Foucault calls the *denegation* of discourse. In broad terms, this challenge relates to the subject matter of Chapter 2, where I described the *linguistic turn* as changing language (or discourse) from being thought of as a medium for expressing meanings that pre-exist linguistic formulation to a system that constitutes meaningfulness in its own terms. Foucault challenges three habits of mind:

a   'that of never treating discourse except as ... a simple site of expression of thoughts, imaginings, knowledges, unconscious themes'

b   that of only seeing in discourse patterns related to the psychological traits of an author, or related to a particular style or genre, or to an idea or theme

c   'that of supposing that all operations are conducted prior to discourse and outside of it, in the ideality of thought or the silent gravity of practices' (pp. 62–3).

4   The fourth is to replace the *uncertainties* Foucault associates with cultural history, or the history of ideas with 'the analysis of discourse itself in its conditions of formation, in its serial modification, and in the play of its dependencies and correlations' with discourses being seen as 'describable' in relation to other practices, including political ones (p. 64).

Such a brief summary does scant justice to the complexity of Foucault's thought. Similar to Bakhtin, however, his rethinking of key concepts is integral to any account of the discursive formation of CDA itself. The sense he attributes to the concept of the 'critical', as he himself has indicated, allows for the highlighting of tensions and incompatibilities in other meanings of the concept, even within the same discursive formation.

Other writers on CDA have a different slant on the object and process of revelation. This approach moves the focus from Foucault's *episteme* to the individual subject operating *within* particular discursive framings – what Wodak calls 'the individual human being as a social individual in response to available "representational resources"' (2001: 6). As this argument goes, subscription to a particular discourse at the individual level is likely to be an *unconsciousness* effect of the processes of discursive formation that occur at the societal level. Discourses are *naturalized* for individual subjects, who, viewing the world through their own discursive lenses, regard their own position as 'common sense' rather than a particular construction of reality. Revelation occurs when these 'common sense' positions are *demystified* or *denaturalized*, and exposed as discursive constructions.

In the CDA literature, this argument is often related to a view of society as characterized by unequal power relations appearing as societal conventions. 'Dominant structures stabilize conventions and naturalize them, that is, the effects of power and ideology in the production of meaning are obscured and acquire stable and natural forms: they are taken as "given"' (ibid.: 3). In terms of this view, CDA has a role in piercing the opacity of these arrangements of structural dominance which, in van Dijk's view, are more powerfully established via the subtle, everyday, textual work of persuasion, dissimulation and manipulation that sets out to change the minds of others in one's own interests (1993: 254).

When Kincheloe and McLaren (1994) describe the 'critical project' as 'the attempt to move beyond assimilated experience, the struggle to expose the way ideology constrains the desire for self-direction, and the effort to confront the way power reproduces itself in the construction of human consciousness' (p. 152) they have in effect distanced themselves from Foucault's distrust of something as stable as an 'ideology' and the sense of power as originating in the agency of particular self-interested groups. They are closer to Althusser's (1971) notion of *ideological state apparatus*, his definition of ideology as representing 'the imaginary relationship of individuals to their real conditions of existence' (p. 153), and the way ideology functions in 'hailing' or *interpellating* 'concrete individuals as concrete subjects' (p. 162). For the individual subject who 'recognises' her or himself as the one who is hailed, the construction of reality embodied in the ideology has already achieved the status of common sense.

Certainly, 'ideology' is a concept that currently resists erasure. 'Even with differing concepts', Wodak (2001), writes, 'critical theory intends to create awareness in agents of how they are deceived about their own needs and interests' (p. 10). Again, a Foucaultian perspective would suspect the tendency in such an utterance to suggest a superior, critical vantage point *outside of* discourse. James Gee, another key figure in the CDA literature, also acknowledges the contested nature of the term, but comes up with his own definition: 'By ideology I mean a social theory which involves generalizations (beliefs, claims) about the way(s) in which goods are distributed in society' (1996: 21).

For my own part, I define an ideology is an elaborate story told about the ideal conduct of some aspect of human affairs. As I see it, its power lies in its truth value, which is determined by the number and nature of its subscription base as much as by some notion of 'explanatory force'. In short, the truth of an ideology is determined by the number subscribing to it. The related term, 'hegemony', can consequently be defined as the state of affairs which exists when the subscription base of an ideology is broad in terms of numbers and reinforced 'vertically' by the social status of its subscribers. Or to put it more stridently, 'Hegemony is secured when the viru-lence of oppression, in its many guises (e.g. race, gender, class, sexual orientation) is accepted as consensus' (Kincheloe and McLaren 1994: 141).

Critical practice as self-reflexive

Reading Foucault one cannot help but be stuck by a tone. Whilst an essay such as 'Politics and the study of dis-course' reveals discourses as complex, self-contradictory and unstable, there is a declarative confidence in the discoverability of the object of his analytical inquiry – the set of rules that for a particular *episteme* determines what can be said and not said. In his own terms, Foucault (despite his avowed distrust of genius) almost single-handedly invented a discourse – cultural archaeology, the science of discourse. For his discursive code-breaking, for revealing an underlying order of things with an emphasis on 'large-scale structures and their underlying principles' (Pennycook 2001: 31), Foucault has sometimes been termed a structuralist. (For his disavowal of such an attribution, see Foucault 1980: 111–15.)

Both postmodernity (as descriptive of a condition) and post-structuralism (as indicating a stance on the act of reading) act to undermine certainty by introducing another kind of critical tendency having a bearing on CDA as a research method. Using the idea of story dis-cussed in Chapter 1, we can think of postmodernity as a condition which erodes confidence in any single story (or grand narrative) as having superior or absolute status as an explanation for anything. Postmodernity offers a pic-ture of cultural viewpoints, discourses, 'takes' on the meaning of life, genres, jostling with one another in a kaleidoscopic mélange susceptible to rapid hybridization and pastiche. In former times, its metaphor might have been the bazaar. In these so-called 'new times' it is the World Wide Web, where another take on things is just a mouse click away. (For a discussion of the distinction between postmodernism and postmodernity – or hyper-reality – see Kincheloe and McLaren 1994: 142–3 and Pennycook 2001. The latter describes postmodernism as calling into question 'any claims to overarching truths such as human nature, enlightenment, or emancipation' and sceptical 'about talk of reality, truth, or universality' (p. 134.))

Post-structuralism, like postmodernism, relates to the *linguistic turn* (see Chapter 2) by suggesting that reality is discursively constructed via human sign systems. One of the thinkers associated with post-structuralism, Jacques Derrida, invented the idea of *différance* to assert a funda-mental instability in textual meaning owing to the play of signs within language. The sense of a stable, underlying order of things suggested by structuralism was replaced by surface interdeterminacy and play. Deconstruction became a procedure for demonstrating ways in which textual meanings are actually *indeterminate*. Now acts of reading are at the heart of CDA. Yet, as Patterson (1997) points out, 'the idea that something resides in texts awaiting extraction, or revelation, by the application of the correct means of interpretation is precisely the assumption that post-structuralism set out to pro-blematise' (p. 427). Post-structuralist reading practices acknowledge the historical situatedness of texts, gaps in textual coherence, the indeterminacy of textual meaning and ways in which texts encapsulate versions of reality (Morgan 1992).

Given such powerful contemporary bases for scepti-cism, it behoves criticalist researchers to be self-reflexive, 'to become aware of the ideological imperatives and epistemological presuppositions that inform their research as well as their own subjective, intersubjective, and normative reference claims' (Kincheloe and McLaren 1994: 140). Kincheloe and McLaren view self-reflexivity as twofold. First, researchers need to acknowledge the social constructedness of their research method. This includes a preparedness to view the 'common sense' meanings of the very terms used as discursively constructed (McLaughlin 1995). Second, researchers need to acknowledge the provisionality of their findings.

Post-structuralism replaces the individual self as originary meaning-maker with the individual subjectivity as the social product of discourse. Whether one views the self as synonymous with subjectivity and multiple, or distinct from subjectivity and singular, is a matter of debate. I represent the relationship between self and discourse dialectically in Figure 3.1, while deliberately allowing for

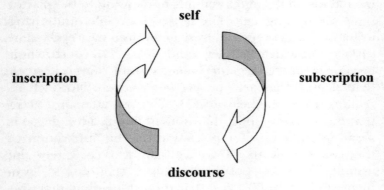

Figure 3.1 Self and discourse

this diagram to be read in different ways. Whatever, provisionality is a necessary outcome of a position which asserts that researchers operate out of a discursively framed and thereby contestable subjectivity. Van Dijk (1993) writes bluntly: 'CDA is unabashedly normative: any critique by definition presupposes an applied ethics' (p. 253). In their overview of qualitative research and critical theory, Kincheloe and McLaren insist that 'The empirical data derived from any study cannot be treated as simple irrefutable facts. They represent hidden assumptions – assumptions the critical researcher must dig out and expose' (1994: 144). The required researcher attitude is modesty or 'reflective humility' (ibid.: 151). And as they further argue, traditional notions of internal and external validity may need to be replaced by something they call *critical trustworthiness* (see ibid.: 151–2 for a discussion of this).

Critical practice as socially transformative

The tendency for critical practice to be linked to a socially transformative agenda stems from a view of discourse (and ideology) as involving power relations. Earlier in this chapter, we saw how Foucault indicated that one of five things discursively constructed by an *archive* is 'The limits and forms of *appropriation*', which is concerned with *who* has access to *what* discourses. A relevant question Foucault notes is: 'How is struggle for control of discourses conducted between classes, nations, linguistic, cultural or ethnic collectivities?' (1991: 60). I have suggested that the power of a discourse relates to its subscription base and the social status of its subscribers. On this basis, some discourses are more powerful than others and subscribers of non-powerful discourses are therefore marginalized and relatively disempowered.

Critical researchers tend to align themselves with a political agenda that is committed to challenging the relative power bases of competing discourses. The *how* of conducting this agenda and the language in which it is couched varies among critical discourse analysts. One school of thought (represented by Ruth Wodak, Teun van Dijk, Michael Meyer and others) relates this aspect of the critical to the notion of *dominance* which is defined as 'the exercise of social power by elites, institutions or groups, that results in social inequality, including political, cultural, class, ethnic, racial and gender inequality'. Such writers view CDA as taking an 'explicit socio-political stance' and bringing about 'change through critical understanding' (van Dijk 1993: 249–50, 252–3).

Specifically, of course, CDA is concerned with the ways in which the power relations produced by discourse are maintained and/or challenged through texts and the practices which affect their production, reception and dissemination. As Wodak (2001) puts it, 'CDA takes an interest in the ways in which linguistic forms are used in various expressions and manipulations of power' (p. 11). One of the motives driving the 'Genre School' in Australia was a view that certain genres be considered genres of power and that schooling ensure that underprivileged students have access to them (Cope and Kalantzis 1993). (Critical literacy advocates in the same country critiqued the 'Genre School' for its supposed failure to recognize the discursively loaded nature of these genres.)

Both critical literacy and critical language awareness can be thought of as pedagogical approaches to literacy committed to bringing about change through critical understanding. The two approaches have much in common with each other (and with critical discourse analysis) but with differing emphases depending on the theorists and practitioners themselves.

Critical literacy, as a number of commentators have pointed out (for example, Lankshear 1994, Morgan 1997) is a contested discourse that comes in various forms. Writing of the Australian variant, Morgan describes critical literacy as 'a view of language and text as always operating within and on, for or against, the inequitable socio-political arrangements of society. Central to its work therefore is the scrutiny of the linguistic and visual forms of representation and the implicit or explicit struggle over meaning within the available signifying systems' (1997: 23). As a reading practice, it tends to be underpinned by the post-structuralist principles discussed previously. Reading a text critically means developing an awareness of how texts mediate and sustain particular discourses and power relations (Lankshear 1994: 10).

Critical language awareness, as an approach to literacy education, shares these assumptions but focuses on the range of textual and non-textual practices in a society that ensure the dominance of a particular discourse (or ideology) (see Fairclough 1992b). Catherine Wallace, for example, who worked with migrant EFL students in London, focused her pedagogy on the nature of the reading practices associated with particular social groups, the influences on textual interpretation in particular contexts and the wider question: 'How is reading material produced in a particular society, that is how do texts such as newspapers, advertisements, leaflets and public information come to us in the form they do, who produces them, and how do they come to have the salience they do?' (1992: 63). Discussing the development of the *Critical Language Awareness Series* of workbooks for students during the time when apartheid was the prevailing ideology in South Africa, Janks (1994) describes CLA as attempting to 'raise awareness of the way in which language can be used (and is used) to maintain and to challenge existing forms of power' (p. 51). So described, CLA is an overt consciousness-raising exercise, concerned to make language-users aware of the verbal and non-verbal choices that are and *can be* made in the production of texts and the ways in which these choices are used to reinforce particular discursive hegemonies.

4

The Question of Metalanguage in CDA

I start this chapter with a sentence: 'A woman was raped yesterday morning in Kingsland'. I imagine this sentence occurring in a news story but it could feasibly occur in other contexts. At one level, this sentence can be thought of as communicating information about an event. (I'm aware that there is disagreement about what constitutes rape.) Similar information would be communicated had this sentence been used: 'Une femme était ravie hier matin en Kingsland'. What I'm drawing attention to here is the mundane miracle of communicability via language. I might refer to it as the *transparency* of an utterance. It is not, however, the primary concern of CDA.

CDA's concern is with the *opacity* of texts and utterances – the discursive constructions or stories that are embedded in texts as information that is less readily available to consciousness. Analysis is a method of dealing with this opacity. In respect of the sentence quoted, we might note that it has a subject ('A woman'), a finite verb ('was raped') and two adverbials indicating when and where the rape occurred ('yesterday morning' and 'in Kingsland'). We can further note that the verb is passive voice. The woman (as subject) is having the action done to her. There is no adverbial to indicate by whom she was raped. In effect, the form of the sentence suppresses information about the perpetrator of the rape. In particular, the rapist's gender is rendered invisible. Going a step further, we might conclude that this sentence *instantiates* a discourse or story about rape where the focus is on the female subject and where the gender of the perpetrators is not of account.

As a researcher, I could conceivably analyse reports of rape across various mass media over a period of time in a particular social setting as a way of gauging the extent to which this discourse is subscribed to. As a social activist, having become aware of this discourse, I might begin a campaign on the basis of a different discourse, perhaps with the slogan: 'Rape is a male problem'.

Relevant to this chapter, however, is the fact that I've drawn on a linguistic toolkit to deal analytically with textual opacity. That is, I've used a *metalanguage* to talk *about* language. I can conduct a similar operation with my Chapter 1 text: 'Kelly Browne's parents are away. PARTY at her place!' The only finite verb we can positively identify is the stative verb 'are'. (*Stative* verbs show qualities incapable of change, whereas *dynamic* verbs show qualities capable of change.) 'Party' *could* be a verb, but it could equally be a noun. What the stative verb adds to the story identified in Chapter 1 is a sense that 'this is the way things are' – you can't change them. This aspect of the story is reinforced by the lack of an identifiable subject *doing* anything in this ad. Kelly Browne herself is significantly absent as an agent.

In this chapter, I examine two related questions.

1   How much linguistic knowledge does one need to do CDA?
2   What or whose linguistic knowledge is useful?

How much

One way of framing this question is to relate it to a commonplace diagram in the CDA literature, Fairclough's three boxes (1995: 98), where he relates his three interrelated dimensions of discourse (see Chapter 1) to three interrelated processes of analysis. What is useful in Fairclough's schematization is that it highlights the socially and discursively embedded nature of any text. It also permits differing foci for analysis:

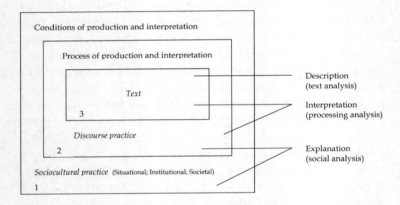

Figure 4.1 Fairclough's dimensions of discourse and discourse analysis.

1   *Sociocultural practice:* a focus on such things as the immediate situation that has given rise to its production and the various sociocultural practices and discursive conditions at both institutional and societal levels that provide a wider contextual relevance.

2   *Discourse practice:* a focus on the way in which the text has been produced, including its relationship with similar texts, its mode of dissemination and the way

in which it is received, read, interpreted and used by human subjects.

3   *Text:* a focus on the text to ascertain ways in which it discursively positions readers via what Janks and Ivanic (1992) term its *preferred* reading.

Analysis at the level of sociocultural practice is aimed at exploring such questions as whether the particular text supports a particular kind of discursive hegemony or a particular social practice, or whether it stands in a counter-hegemonic relationship to certain prevalent conditions. Does it serve to reproduce particular social and discursive practices, or are there transformative impulses in the text?

Analysis at the level of discourse practice focuses on aspects of a text's production, distribution and consumption (or reception/interpretation). Drawing on and simplifying Fairclough (1992a: 232–4):

- A focus on text production raises questions about both *interdiscursivity* and *manifest intertextuality.* The former is concerned with the way in which a text appears to subscribe to one or more discourses (e.g. discourses related to partying and parenting in the Kelly Browne ad). The latter is concerned with the way in which other texts are utilized in the construction of a given text (e.g. the Tony Brown parody referred to in Chapter 1).

- A focus on text distribution raises questions about the way a given text becomes part of an *intertextual chain* in being transformed into other text-types. For example, the Kelly Browne ad entered into an intertextual chain with a series of television ads and other texts which were part of an overall advertising campaign.

- A focus on text interpretation raises questions about what Fairclough rather confusingly terms *coherence.* What he is referring to here I would prefer to call *reader disposition,* that is, the extent to which readers (the target as

43

well as non-target audience) are disposed to subscribe to a text's 'preferred' reading and, in general, how readers *actually* respond to a text.

One might observe crudely that the third of Fairclough's three foci is the province of critical linguistics, the first of cultural ethnography and sociology, and the second a hybridization of all of these academic traditions. Such an observation reflects the extent to which CDA is an inter-disciplinary enterprise. However, it is the third of these foci which calls for linguistic knowledge or a metalanguage.

The simple answer to the question 'How much knowledge?' is: enough to ascertain the reading position a particular text/utterance appears to be (covertly) offering its readers/viewers/listeners. As Janks (1997) shows via a specific textual demonstration, texts vary in what I have called their opacity. Moreover, the discursive workings of certain kinds of linguistic patterning (for example, transitivity) are more opaque than others. As a way of addressing the above question, I outline two approaches to the question of metalanguage, before moving to some specific analyses of my own in Chapters 5 and 6. However, readers may take comfort from Fairclough's observation that 'discourse analysis is in fact a multidisciplinary activity, and one can no more assume a detailed linguistic background from its practitioners than one can assume detailed backgrounds in sociology, psychology, or politics' (1992a: 74).

Hallidayan grammar via Fairclough

Ruth Wodak (2001) asserts that 'an understanding of the basic claims of Halliday's grammar [i.e. systemic functional grammar] and his approach to linguistic analysis is essential for a proper understanding of CDA' (p. 8). In this section, I allow myself to be interpellated by this claim and provide a brief account of Halliday's approach and Fairclough's adaptation of it for CDA purposes.

In Chapter 2, I outlined Halliday's framework for describing the *context of situation* – the social context of a text which allowed for meaning to be exchanged – and his use of the terms *field, tenor* and *mode*. The name for Halliday's grammar – *systemic functional* – derives from a view of *function* as a 'fundamental property of language itself, something that is basic to the evolution of the semantic system' (Halliday and Hasan 1985: 17). Halliday distinguished three metafunctions of language:

1   The *ideational* which he further divided into:
    a   The *experiential*, which constructs a version of or gives meaning to our experience.
    b   The *logical* which defines 'the relationship between one process and another, or one participant and another, that share the same position in the text' (ibid.: 45).
2   The *interpersonal* which defines the process of social interaction which is occurring.
3   The *textual* which denotes the interplay and relationship of linguistic elements which gives a text its coherence.

In relationship to the context of situation, Halliday argued that the field was generally expressed through the experiential function, the tenor through the interpersonal function and the mode through the textual function.

In his social theory of discourse (1992a), Fairclough adopted these three metafunctions but split the interpersonal into an *identity* function (concerned with the construction of social identity and subjectivity) and a *relational* function (concerned with the way in which relationships between people are constructed). He organized *text analysis* under four main headings, forming a kind of ascending scale (small units to bigger ones). This organization is represented in Table 4.1. To the seven

Table 4.1 Fairclough: text analysis

Text analysis			
Vocabulary	Grammar	Cohesion	Text Structure
Deals mainly with individual words. • word meaning • wording • metaphor	Deals with words combined into clauses and sentences. • modality • transitivity and theme	Deals with how clauses and sentences are linked together • connectives and argumentation	Deals with large-scale organizational properties. • interactional control

bulleted textual properties, which can be viewed as a checklist, Fairclough added further properties of *politeness* and *ethos* – making nine features in all. I will be following Fairclough's logic is discussing each of these features in turn. For a fuller discussion, readers are referred to Fairclough (1992a) and Halliday (1994). For absolute beginners who would like a well written, succinct account of Hallidayan grammar, I recommend Beverley Derewianka's *A Grammar Companion for Primary Teachers* (1998).

Four of Fairclough's nine analytical properties are especially concerned with the relational and identity functions of language, which together make up the interpersonal metafunction.

1   *Interactional control:* related to text structure, this property is concerned with such things as turn-taking, the selection and change of topics, the control of the agenda and how interactions are

established and finished. An analysis of interactional control in an oral speech genre, for example, can be revealing about the power relations that are being constituted across a sequence of utterances.

2 *Modality:* related to grammar, this property refers to the strength with which a particular proposition or statement is endorsed. This can be shown through the use of *modal auxiliary verbs* such as 'may' and 'should', but can also be shown by the absence of a modal auxiliary and by the use of modal adverbs such as 'possibly' and 'clearly'. 'Kelly Browne's parents are away' is an example of a 'categorical' modality. The ad's impact would be different had the sentence read: 'Kelly Browne's parents may be away'.

3 *Politeness* relates to the property of force. Force is concerned with the nature of particular speech acts, whether they are promises, declarations, requests, threats, and so on. Both these terms come from a branch of linguistics known as pragmatics, which has a broad interest in the relationship of language to context. Politeness is built around the idea that participants in an interaction tend to operate in ways that ensure that no party 'loses face'. What CDA adds to this idea is the sense that particular politeness conventions implicitly evince particular social and power relations.

4 *Ethos* is related to the 'sorts of social identity [people] implicitly signal through their verbal and non-verbal comportment'. To illustrate this feature, Fairclough uses the example of a medical practitioner who sets out to make his surgery more 'homely' by rearranging furniture and changing the décor (1992a: 166).

Fairclough connects five of his nine analytical properties

with the ideational metafunction of language and the way this constitutes, reproduces, challenges and restructures systems of knowledge and belief in discourse.

5   *Connectives and argumentation* are related to cohesion. Fairclough points out that text types differ in the way their clauses relate to one another and in the sorts of cohesion they favour. These differences, he argues, can have cultural or ideological significance. Fairclough draws on Halliday in distinguishing three main types of relation between clauses: elaboration, extension and advancement (see Halliday 1994: 196–7). He also draws on Halliday in distinguishing four main types of explicit cohesive marking:

a   *Reference*: using personal pronouns, demonstratives and so on to refer to something earlier or later in a text.

b   *Substitution and ellipsis*: 'William put out the rubbish. Isn't he a good boy!' is an example of substitution where 'William' is replaced by the equivalent 'boy'. In the example: 'I went to the bank to draw out some money, but there wasn't any', there is an ellipsis of 'money' in the second half of the sentence.

c   *Conjunction*: conjunctions such as 'and' and 'because' and conjunctive expressions such as 'in other words' are used to achieve cohesion.

d   *Lexical cohesion*: this refers to such devices as word repetition and the use of *synonyms* and *collocations* (i.e. words that are associated with each other in common usage, e.g. fish and chips).

6   *Transitivity* and *theme* are both related to grammar. Transitivity is the ideational dimension of the grammar of the clause and is concerned with the

types of processes and elements that are coded in clauses. Transitivity is a key focus in CDA. Fairclough distinguishes four types of process:

a   *Relational:* the verb marks a relationship (being, having, becoming, and so on) between participants, e.g. '100 demonstrators are dead' (Fairclough's example).

b   *Action:* an agent acts upon a goal. This is usually shown in a transitive (subject–verb–object [SVO]) clause, e.g. 'The police shot 100 demonstrators'. The latter is an action process in the active voice. In passive voice, the goal becomes the subject and the agent is either passive (named in a phrase beginning with 'by') or omitted, e.g. '100 demonstrators were shot (by police)'. As Fairclough (1992a) points out, 'an issue which is always important is whether agency, causality and responsibility are made explicit or left vague in media accounts of important events' (p. 181).

c   *Event:* this involves an event and a goal and is usually conveyed in intransitive (subject–verb [SV]) clauses, e.g. '100 demonstrators died'.

d   *Mental:* these processes include verbs of knowing (e.g. 'think'), perceiving (e.g. 'hear) and feeling ('enjoy') and are usually realized as transitive clauses, e.g. 'The demonstrators feared the police'.

In his discussion of this property, Fairclough includes two other aspects of grammar. The first is the Hallidayan concept of *theme*, the initial part of a clause which gives prominence to particular information and which, in CDA terms, is often an indication of taken-for-granted or 'common sense' assumptions about the nature of things. The second is *nominalization*, which refers to the process

49

by which processes are converted into nouns or noun phrases. An example would be changing 'A woman was raped in Kingsland' to 'A rape occurred in Kingsland.' As can be seen, the process of nominalization in this example allows for the elision of both agent *and* goal.

7   *Word meaning* relates to vocabulary. In his discussion, Fairclough notes that the same word can have a number of different meanings. This multiplicity of meanings he refers to as a word's *meaning potential*. He also challenges assumptions behind the 'dictionary' meaning of a word that suggest a *stability* of meaning potential and a lack of contradiction *between* meanings. Rather, he argues, the meanings ascribed to a word in accordance with its meaning potential are often contestable. In other words, shifts in word meanings can be a key indicator of discursive contestation and subtle changes in discursive formation. In a similar vein, Dale (1989) uses the term *sense legitimation* to describe a strategy for manufacturing consent in a group and thereby achieving the hegemony of a discourse. The strategy involves couching potentially unpopular policy changes, for example, in words whose meanings have been subtly changed. In my own work in education, I have analysed ways in which 'reforms' have been more readily effected by subtle shifts in the discursive construction of such words as 'professional' (Locke 2001).

8   *Wording* also relates to vocabulary, referring to the various ways a meaning can be 'worded'. The 'same' experience or object will be *worded* differently from perspectives which are differently discursively framed. One person's 'asylum seeker' is another person's 'queue jumper'; one person's 'terrorist' is another person's 'freedom-fighter'. As far as CDA is

concerned, it is clear that particular wordings are clues to interdiscursive relationships between texts. Arguably, the more frequently a particular wording is taken up across a range of texts in a range of situations, the more likely it is that a particular discourse is enlarging its subscription base.

9 Fairclough's last property, *metaphor*, is also related to vocabulary. The term embraces such 'figures of speech' as *simile, personification* and *metonymy*. As Fairclough notes, 'Metaphors structure the way we think and the way we act, and our systems of knowledge and belief, in a pervasive and fundamental way' (1992a: 194). As with wording, the metaphorization of an area of experience is contestable. Saddam Hussain may be described as a 'butcher' or a 'patriarch of his people' depending on one's discursive frame. Once particular metaphors become naturalized within a particular cultural or institutional setting, they tend to become invisible. At different times and in different contexts, for example, educational systems have become naturalized as either factories, gardens or business enterprises. In such instances, education itself is being constructed in radically different ways with radically different effects.

Alternative categories: James Gee

For Gee (1996) the primary purpose of CDA is to make *explicit* the Discourses (which he habitually capitalizes) embedded in texts which would otherwise remain implicit, invisible and thereby all the more powerful. At one point in his book *Social Linguistics and Literacies: Ideology in Discourses,* he notes that a key way humans think about the world is through seeking out similarities. He asks his readers to consider the rather innocuous-sounding sentence: 'The teacher taught the students French.' He notes that this sentence has a similar construction to such sentences as 'John handed Mary the gun', 'John gave Mary the gun', 'John sent Mary the gun', and many more. He goes on to suggest that 'This type of sentence seems to mean (if we consider prototypical cases like "give", "hand", and "send") that an agent transfers something to someone.'

> We are led to think of teaching French as transferring something (French) from one person (the teacher) to someone else (the student), though this transfer is a mental one, rather than a physical one. This suggestion (about the meaning of teaching languages), which we pick up from our grammar, happens to fit with one of the most pervasive ways of thinking (what I will later call a master myth) embedded in our language and in culture. We tend to think of meaning as something speakers or writers take out of their heads (its original container), package, like a gift, into a package or container (i.e., words and sentences) and convey (transfer) to hearers, who unpackage it and place its contents (i.e., 'meaning') into their heads (its final container). (p. 71)

Gee relates this container/conveyer metaphor to idiomatic expressions such as 'I catch your meaning', 'I can't grasp what you are saying' and 'I've got it'. The idiomatic embeddedness of this metaphor of a conveyor belt to construct the teaching of language gives it the power of common sense and makes it harder to contest. Gee uses his example to show the way language encapsulates what he calls 'frozen theories'. CDA exposes such theories to scrutiny and potential contestation.

For analytical purposes, Gee views language in use as made up of five interrelated linguistic systems (in contrast with Fairclough's nine properties) which together constitute the *sensefulness* of a text (p. 93). He characterizes the five systems as follows:

1   *Prosody*: 'The ways in which the words and sentences of a text are said: their pitch, loudness, stress, and the length assigned to various syllables, as well as the way in which the speaker hesitates and pauses' (p. 94).

2   *Cohesion*: 'The multifarious linguistic ways in which sentences are connected to each other. It is the "glue" that holds texts together' (p. 94). This system parallels Hallidayan cohesion.

3   *Discourse organization*: 'The ways in which sentences are organised into higher-order units (bigger than single sentences), for example, the scenes and episodes making up a story or the arguments and sub-arguments making up an overall argument for a particular position' (p. 94).

4   *Contextualization signals*: the 'cues' by which speakers and writers indicate and to some extent negotiate the immediate situation of the text's production.

5   *Thematic organization*: 'The ways in which themes (images, contrasts, focal points of interest) are signalled and developed' (p. 94).

In offering Gee's checklist, I am emphasizing the fact that CDA has more than one checklist and grammatical system available to it for purposes of textual analysis. A reader interested in the application of Gee's procedure should check out his analysis of an argument by a young, adult, lower-middle class, Jewish woman from Philadelphia (pp. 93–103). In Chapter 5, I turn to my own analysis of a newspaper editorial. In it, I model the use of Gee's checklist. I model the use of Fairclough's properties in Chapter 6.

5

Analysing a Print Text

In this chapter, I offer a close analysis of a print text. In keeping with my concluding remarks to Chapter 1, this analysis will be concerned with language in use and the way in which patterns of meaning as socially constructed versions of reality – discourses – are embedded and disseminated in texts. It will be critical because a central concern of the act of analysis will be to highlight the potential social effects of the meanings that a reader of a text is positioned or called upon (*interpellated*) to subscribe to. Box 5.1 is a newspaper editorial, entitled 'A matter of attitude', published on 31 October 1997 in the *New Zealand Herald*, an Auckland-based daily with the largest circulation in the country.

A focus on sociocultural practice

The immediate situation prompting this editorial was the Māori school drop-out rate in Northland, the most northerly region of New Zealand. Its focus is the relative educational non-achievement of Māori, the indigenous people of New Zealand, in the mainstream schooling system. A number of statistics are quoted to support the editorial's concerns. Readers with scant knowledge of New Zealand are likely to be unaware of the social context of this editorial. Relevant information would include some knowledge of Māori–European (Pakeha) relations in New Zealand/Aotearoa since the days of first contact; the struggle of the Māori to establish a parallel education system operating according to Māori tikanga (customs); and information about Northland itself, a region of the country which attracts many tourists but is poor in socio-economic terms. In 1996, a year before the editorial's publication, the official Māori unemployment rate of 19 per cent was three times that of non-Māori (6 per cent). In Northland, however, the unemployment rate for Māori was the highest in New Zealand (24 per cent) (Te Puni Kokori 1999). Another factor not mentioned in the editorial is the black market economy in marijuana in Northland and the high incidence of marijuana dependence among Māori compared with non-Māori.

One can identify a number of discourses available to the editorial writer as he/she addresses the causes of Māori educational failure. Some of these are race-related. While New Zealand often projects an image of itself as a racially harmonious society, there is no compelling reason to expect its media to be exempt from the racist discourses reported by van Dijk (1991) as suffusing Western media.

> Most blatantly in the past and usually more subtly today, the Press has indeed been a main 'foe' of black and other minorities ... Until today, its dominant definition of ethnic affairs has consistently been a negative and stereotypical one: minorities or immigrants are seen as a problem or a threat, and are portrayed preferably in association with crime, violence, conflict, unacceptable cultural differences, or other forms of deviance. While paying extensive attention to these racialized or ethnicized forms of problems or conflict, it failed to pay attention to the deeper social, political, or economic causes and backgrounds to these conflicts. (pp. 20–1)

Other available discourses more particularly relate to

education itself. Different discourses construct educational failure differently. Some construct it in terms of an inappropriate or badly designed curriculum; some in terms of ineffective pedagogy. A common one – the 'deficit' model – constructs school failure as arising from certain (cultural) deficiencies in the home of the failing child. This discourse has a long history in the Western world, so one would expect to find it in the New Zealand setting.

Box 5.1   *Herald* editorial: 'A matter of attitude'

A matter of attitude

(1)   One of the more telling observations in a three-year study on Maori educational performance in Northland states: 'I see primary-age children, all Maori, pushing their parents' trolleys around the supermarket at 11 am on a Friday – and they're not sick.'

(2)   The research reveals a tragic and disturbing cycle of intergenerational ignorance and confirms what has long been suspected: among Northland Maori there is an appalling school drop-out rate.

(3)   If the realities exposed by Oneroa Stewart are to be reversed it will require a degree of honesty and candour that is rarely evident in such matters. The first point to be faced is that educational failure is mostly, although not exclusively, a problem for Maori.

(4)   Maori make up 45 per cent of the Northland secondary school population. Just 11 per cent of Northland Maori students complete their seventh-form year compared with 18 per cent Maori nationally, and 46 per cent of all students. And the situation is actually getting worse than those statistics reveal because many Maori students drop out of school long before reaching the seventh form.

(5)   Mr Stewart, a doctoral student at Auckland University, finds that nearly half the Maori boys in Northland have disappeared from school by the end of the fourth

---

form. They leave not to work but to join the huge and growing pool of unemployed – and unemployable. They have no skills and an education that is barely adequate for day-to-day survival in the modern world.

(6) The study suggests some remedies that schools should attempt, such as employing a visiting teacher for face-to-face interviews with parents. Yet it is not schools, teaching methods, or the curriculum that is the problem – it is the attitude of Maori parents and the Maori community that is being passed on from generation to generation.

(7) Apologists, of whom there are far too many, will make nebulous claims that the education system is failing Maori. Nonsense. Maori are failing Maori. All the specialist measures that are conceived will not make a jot of difference to the Northland educational tragedy until Maori can turn around the attitude of Maori to education. In fact, various special measures risk doing more harm than good because they divert resources and skills from addressing the underlying cause.

(8) The fact is that most Maori parents in Northland put little value on education and inculcate their children similarly. As Mr Stewart observes, there are high levels of Maori student absenteeism, including condoned truancy. There is absolutely no reason why Northland Maori children cannot achieve at school if they have the will to do so and parents who accord education the same priority as do many parents from other ethnic and socio-economic groups.

(9) A change in attitude towards education needs the collective will of Maoridom. The children need role models they respect to push the cause of education. Maori leaders and organisations need to apply the same energy to improving the next generation's learning as is being given to the grievance industry.

(10) Unless they do the generational cycle of failure will continue.

A focus on text

In this section, I analyse the text proper using the headings proposed by Gee (1996) and discussed in Chapter 4. These headings are: 1. Prosody; 2. Cohesion; 3. Discourse organization; 4. Con-textualization signals; and 5. Thematic organization. In accordance with the self-reflexivity strictures discussed in Chapter 3, I must reiterate that this analysis is an act of interpretation and therefore subject to contestation and critique. Box 5.1 is the full text of the editorial reprinted in this chapter. Paragraph numbers have been inserted for ease of reference.

1 Prosody

Obviously, this editorial is a written piece. However, if we read it with our ears, it is clear that the writer is using certain print equivalents of the devices of an orator. The pregnant pause, for example, can be heard in paragraph 5 in the dash following the word 'unemployed' and in paragraph 6 after the word 'problem'. The latter pause is a key one because it constitutes the fulcrum of an antithesis (where the writer is comparing a *naive* view of the problem with his/her enlightened view). A similar function is served by the one-word sentence 'Nonsense' in paragraph 7. It can be thought of as an emphatic, voiced pause serving also as the fulcrum of an antithesis, which again contrasts the naive view of the problem with the editorial writer's view.

These antitheses are rhetorically designed to underline a central binary opposition in this editorial: the perceptiveness and authority of the writer and the naiveté and dubious authority of other observers. (Binary oppositions are words or concepts that have been constructed as opposed, for example, black and white, rational and emotional, mind and body. Often one particular 'pole' is privileged in a discourse and the other 'pole' contemned or suppressed. CDA allows for binaries to be exposed and contested.)

2 Contextualization signals

This is the fourth of Gee's systems. However, I find it convenient to discuss it at this juncture.

One verbal indicator of the prosodic feature of *stress* is the use of intensifiers. There are a number of these in this editorial, including the words 'long' in the phrase 'long been suspected' (paragraph 2); 'rarely' (paragraph 3); 'actually' (paragraph 4); 'barely' (paragraph 5); 'far', 'a jot of' (paragraph 7) and 'absolutely' (paragraph 8). To these we might add the intensifying adverbial phrase, 'In fact' (paragraph 7) and the intensifying main clause 'The fact is' (paragraph 8). Collectively, these emphatically intensify the writer's argument, reinforcing his/her authority by a form of reiteration.

We don't know who the writer is, of course. And we should be cautious about attributing to him/her a single voice, though I'm talking as if there *is* a single voice coming through this editorial. In keeping with the purpose of CDA, I'm more concerned with the *complex* of discourses speaking through him/her.

These intensifiers have a role in evoking the context of this editorial. As Gee points out, the context is not a given but something constructed in the act of textual engagement. Putting it another way, the writer positions us to view the participants in this situation in a certain way. As mentioned, *he/she* is presented as an insightful and authoritative seer, with the role of 'revealing' (a word I will be coming back to) 'what has long been suspected'. *Our* role is complementary. We are the receivers of the 'truth' he/she is concerned to deliver.

The construction of the context serves to represent

other participants in particular ways also. Another intensifying main clause (introducing a noun clause) occurs in paragraph 3 – 'The first point to be faced is'. This clause highlights another aspect of how the writer wants to be seen – not just as a seer but as a courageous and outspoken truth-sayer who calls a spade a spade. Thus projected, the writer suggests an additional binary opposition between him/herself and those shallow and cowardly commentators – those 'apologists' who make 'nebulous' claims (for example, that the fault may lie with the education system).

So far, we have three categories of participant: the writer, readers and those naive commentators whose 'nonsense' must be disregarded. Another important participant is the researcher, Oneroa Stewart. The editorial writer boosts his/her authority by directly quoting Stewart and mentioning the statistical data in the latter's report. Mr Stewart is described as a 'doctoral student at Auckland University' but there is no mention of his ethnicity. (A Māori name in the New Zealand context does not necessarily indicate Māori ethnicity.) However, it is in paragraph 6 that the writer's real purpose is revealed. With the use of the adverb 'Yet', the writer is distanced from the remedies suggested by Stewart, who is effectively consigned to that group characterized as naive and misguided.

There are other participants who are positioned by the way the writer constructs the context within which he is writing. These include Māori parents, non-Māori parents and Māori leaders and organizations. These are discussed below.

3 Cohesion

Cohesive links 'are part of what stitches a text together into a meaningful whole; they are like threads that tie language, and, thus, also, sense together' (Gee 1996: 97). These devices include conjunctions, pronouns, demonstratives, ellipsis, various adverbs and repeated words and phrases. Let's look at a number of these.

Conjunctions Conjunctions serve to establish relationships of either co-ordination or subordination.

- *And*: co-ordinating conjunctions tend to suggest parallelism. Paragraph 2 begins with a compound sentence which is separated by a colon from a simple statement. The subject of the sentence – 'The research' (of Oneroa Stewart) – does two parallel things: (1) It 'reveals a tragic and disturbing cycle of inter-generational ignorance and (2) confirms what has long been suspected: among Northland Māori there is an appalling school drop-out rate.' The use of 'and', which suggests a similarity in these two 'revelations', actually conceals a logical subordination of cause and effect. Revelation (2) can be established factually. Revelation 1, however, interprets the Māori drop-out rate back to a cause. Is this Stewart's interpretation? Or is it the editorial writer's?
- *If*: conjunctions such as 'if' and 'because' are often used to establish subordinating cause–effect type relationships. In paragraph 3, the effect (the reversal of 'the realities' Stewart's research exposes) will be established by the exercise of 'honesty and candour' (cause) – which, fortunately, this editorial writer has in abundance. In paragraph 8, the effect (Māori scholastic achievement) depends on Māori will-power and parental prioritization. As illogically argued in paragraph 4, the exacerbation of Māori scholastic non-achievement (effect) is a result of young Māori dropping out of school 'long before reaching the seventh form'.

61

Pronouns 'Māori students' (in paragraph 4) are linked to 'Māori boys' (in the first sentence of paragraph 5). In paragraph 5, the pronoun 'They' links the last two sentences to the first. The word Māori appears five times in paragraphs 4 and 5 before it is taken up by the repetition of 'they'. With seven pointed references, it's clear that this is, indeed, a Māori problem.

Listing Argumentation often utilizes lists. If we make a statement and follow it up with a number of reasons, we might say 'first' or 'second'. In paragraph 3 there is the sentence: 'The first point to be faced is that educational failure is mostly, although not exclusively, a problem for Māori.' We are led to expect a series of points about the Māori drop-out rate. After all, the word 'first' has established a platform for the enumeration of various causes for this problem. However, there are no second or third points made – hence a kind of *dis-cohesion*. The reason is clear, as we realize that this writer has eyes for only one cause of the problem – a cause he/she wants to locate fairly and squarely with the Māori themselves.

Auxiliaries The auxiliary 'will' occurs four times in this editorial, in paragraph 3, in paragraph 7 (twice) and in paragraph 10. It is worth considering some of the auxiliaries the writer *might* have used, and thereby changed the verb modality. If we substitute the future form 'is/are going to' or the more conditional 'may', the tenor of these sentences changes dramatically. The repetition of 'will' suggests conviction (a tone of authority) as opposed to tentativeness.

Words in general The following are some of the key words repeated, thereby setting up a complex web of connectedness throughout the text:

- 'attitude' (headline, paragraphs 6, 9)
- 'parents' (paragraphs 1, 6[× 2], 8[× 3])
- 'generation/s/ational' (paragraphs 2, 6[× 2], 9, 10)
- 'cycle' (paragraphs 2, 10)
- 'trag/ic/edy' (paragraphs 2, 7)

Clearly, the situation is hopeless, with the problem neatly identified as psychological and ethical ('a matter of attitude'), of tragic proportions (but like tragedy, associated with the conduct of flawed human beings), inevitable (the hand of fate in tragedy and the sense of cyclical repetition) and endemic to families and patterns of family relationships.

Suppressed is any mention of the opposite poles of these binaries. The following words are *absent*.

- economical situation
- political leaders and government strategists
- structural reforms
- chain of damaging events
- com/ic/edy

Marginalized are stories that view the Māori drop-out problem in terms of structurally induced poverty, governmental policy decisions and (specifically) the wholesale restructuring which occurred in New Zealand in the 1980s and 1990s that changed it from a welfare state to a market-driven economy. There is no place for the recognition of specific events (for example, factory closures and falling returns for primary produce). Nor is there any room for the comic world of free human agency and happy endings. (However, we will see that there *is* an unresolved binary in this editorial between determinism and free will.)

4 Discourse organization

In analysing cohesion, we have focused on the linkages within and between sentences. In looking at the discourse organization (or structure) of this editorial, we are concerned with the ways in which sentences cohere into larger units (in this case paragraphs) and with the organization of the paragraphs themselves. A structural plotting of this editorial might be represented thus (the numbers denote paragraphs):

1   Vignette: a concrete illustration to highlight the general problem.
2   Statement of general thesis: (Māori) 'intergenerational ignorance' is a tragic problem.
3   First solution to problem: in abstract terms this is 'honesty and candour', plus example – a reformulation of the thesis that this is a 'Māori' problem.
4   Statement of evidence for thesis: concrete catalogue of statistics.
5   Further concrete evidence provided to support general thesis.
6   Possible remedies (1) advanced and refuted: restatement of general thesis.
7   Possible remedies (2) advanced and refuted: restatement of general thesis.
8   Another restatement of thesis + evidence for thesis + advancement of second solution.
9   Restatement of second solution.
10 An assertion of belief that this tragic problem will continue if the writer's solution is not adopted.

A number of things become clear when we highlight the discourse organization in this way.

● The rhetorical strategy being employed relies heavily

on statement or assertion. The major thesis (the Māori drop-out rate poses a severe problem; Māori have an attitude problem) is asserted in five out of ten paragraphs.

- As paragraph 2 indicates, this thesis has two prongs: 1) There is a serious drop-out rate; 2) There is a Māori attitude problem. Evidence is provided for the first prong in two paragraphs (drawing on Stewart's study). Evidence for the second prong, which is the major thesis statement, is more scant. An attempt to provide evidence for it is found only in paragraph 8. Even here, the evidence is weak since *condoned* truancy is only a part of the total truancy picture and the writer has not indicated how *big* a part it is.
- Part of the editorial writer's stance is to position him/ herself as a revealer of *causes* rather than advocate for superficial and ineffectual *remedies*. The editorial mentions 'special measures' and 'remedies' but cites only one example of these (visiting teachers). These remedies are viewed as ineffectual because they connect the problem (Māori scholastic non-achievement) with such potential causes as schools, teaching methods and the nature of the curriculum. These potential causes are barely entertained before being dismissed without the provision of any evidence at all.
- The rhetorical structure of the argument tends to present the causes of Māori educational 'failure' as fitting into a neat home/school binary. Whereas the researcher has clearly allowed for school-based causes, the editorial writer is determined to locate the cause in the home. However, as the discussion with respect to cohesion has shown, the reduction of causality to such a binary suppresses any consideration of other kinds of causality (e.g. structurally induced poverty, economic reforms, colonization, and so on).

5 Thematic organization

I have already mentioned a number of themes this editorial develops. In the following discussion, I will simply identify some examples of what I would term *motifs* and show how they underpin the discursive structure of this editorial and advance its position.

- *Hallowing the fact-finder*: the following words (numbers in brackets indicate the paragraphs they occur in) form a thematic cluster: 'observations' (1), 'see' (1), 'reveals' (2), 'exposed' (3), 'reveal' (4), 'finds' (5) 'underlying cause' (7) and 'observes' (8). They suggest a particular relationship to experience – close observation leading to finding/revealing/exposing an underlying causality. I would call this a popular or naive scientific discourse because it also suggests that 'truth' is something out there *in* phenomena waiting to be unearthed ('exposed') rather than something constructed.

  The editorial writer clearly aligns himself with this discourse and uses it as a platform from which other sorts of observers (and their positions) can be attacked. Hence the attack on (by implication, *non-scientific*) 'apologists' and their 'nebulous' claims. The word 'nebulous' suggests a kind of fuzziness in thinking which is in contrast to the hard-edged truth-telling of science.

  As one might expect of a proponent of the empirical method, this editorial writer is hot on facts. The word occurs twice, in paragraphs 7 and 8. The irony, however, is that in both instances the word prefaces the assertion of what are (in fact) opinions: the first that 'special measures risk doing more harm than good'; the second that 'most Māori parents in Northland put little value on education'.

- *A deficit model of education*: the verb 'need/s' is repeated in each sentence in paragraph 9. Repetition, as well as being a cohesive device, is being used for powerful rhetorical effect. The word 'need' positions readers of this editorial to view Māori as operating in terms of a deficit model of culture. Foregrounded is a notion of Māori insufficiency. Suppressed, in terms of this binary, is any sense of Māori sufficiency.

- *Pulling yourself up by your boot straps*: another thematic cluster – 'turn around' (7), 'achieve' (8), 'will' (8), 'will' (9), 'push' (9), 'energy' (9), 'industry' (9) – occurs towards the end of the text, where editorial writers, having stated and analysed a problem, generally advocate a course of action. The phrasal verb 'turn around' is a recognizable neo-liberal, economic discourse *marker*. It's what poorly performing businesses do (often through 'restructuring') when their profits are declining. Here it is being applied to a race, which is poorly performing in the educational sector.

What these Māori parents clearly need is the 'energy', 'will' and 'industry' of those old-fashioned capitalist entrepreneurs who pulled themselves up by their bootstraps and 'achieved' success. What this particular discourse discounts is any sense that the current situation is *not* a 'level playing field'. There is no tolerance for such concepts as 'disadvantage' or 'structural poverty'.

There is, though, an unresolved binary underpinning this editorial – the traditional one between free will and determinism. On the one hand, with its reference to tragedy and a generational cycle, the editorial suggests a picture of inexorability and inevitability. On the other hand, with its adoption of the discourse of capitalistic free enterprise, it suggests a solution which calls on the exercise of individual free will.

- *After all, we are all equal*: in paragraph 8, the editorial neatly establishes a binary between Māori parents and 'parents from other ethnic and socio-economic groups'. It contributes to the argument that there is 'absolutely no reason' why young Māori shouldn't succeed at school, if only *their* parents were like other parents. Māori parents are different in their attitude to education from other parents (whom they should aspire to emulate). In this case, difference should submit to sameness.

To sum up, this editorial addresses Māori non-achievement in the mainstream educational system of New Zealand as indicated by conventional measures of scholastic achievement. The reader is positioned to regard the editorial writer as a courageous and outspoken commentator who is prepared to challenge those *other* naïve, shallow and cowardly 'apologists' who represent contrasting views. In a number of ways, the cause of Māori non-achievement is identified as a problem *for* and *in* Māori themselves. The real cause is neither social nor systemic. It is not to be located in the schooling system, nor in social changes brought about through such agencies as economic restructuring nor colonization. Rather, the problem is psychological and ethical – the result of a failing in Māori themselves, particularly Māori parents. Indeed, the writer, in comparing Māori with other ethnic groups, appears to be suggesting that the race itself is flawed in a certain respect. In terms of educational theory, the discourse propounded here is a deficit model, which locates the cause of non-achievement in the home of the pupil.

A focus on discourse practice

As discussed in Chapter 4, analysis at the level of dis-course practice focuses on aspects of a text's production, distribution and consumption. This level connects the micro-level of a particular text (in this case an editorial) with the macro-level of the socio-cultural context. It looks in particular at issues of interdiscursivity and manifest intertextuality in the production of texts – ways in which texts become links in intertextual chains in acts of dis-tribution; and ways in which they are *received* by their readership or audience. Interdiscursivity has been dis-cussed in the previous two sections of this chapter. In this section, I make some general points about the editorial as genre, manifest intertextuality, intertextual chains and text interpretation.

According to van Dijk (1991), 'the mass media have nearly exclusive control over the symbolic resources needed to manufacture popular consent, especially in the domain of ethnic relations' (p. 43). Newspapers can be thought of as compendia of particular genres (see Chapter 2). Of these, news stories, headlines, editorials, opinion pieces, columns, political cartoons and feature articles can be prime loci for the discursive deployment of these 'symbolic resources'. A newspaper editorial is characterized by its privileging in terms of location, its typical anonymity (the writer's identity is usually sup-pressed) and its rhetorical purpose – to convey the newspaper's carefully weighed viewpoint on a topical issue. It uses various means to establish the authority of its argument, for example, by recourse to statistics and the views of others. Its structure typically commences with an introduction to the topic (for example, through a vign-ette), proceeds to a number of argued points (for or against one or more central propositions) and concludes with a judgement or call to action. Its diction is formal but plain. Its syntax is often complex and rhetorically balanced as befits its argumentative purpose.

Manifest intertextuality occurs when another text is overtly drawn upon in the construction of a particular text. Such is the case with Box 5.1, which quotes from the study of Oneroa Stewart. Key issues for a discourse analyst are *how* a text is used and the effect of this usage. In this text, quoting scholarly research serves the editorial writer's desire to appear authoritative. However, we have already noted that the writer parts company with Mr Stewart over issues of causality and solutions. This parting of the ways occurs more than half-way through the editorial, though, and a casual reader (who might also assume Mr Stewart to be a Māori on the basis of his first name) would be tempted to assume that the researcher and the writer share a similar position.

Newspapers, of course, are more likely to attract casual readers than university doctoral students. For the six months to 30 September 2002, the *Herald*'s average net circulation was 211, 246, more than twice the circulation of any other daily newspaper in New Zealand and 47 per cent of the country's total metropolitan newspaper circulation. (It is generally regarded as a conservative, right-wing paper and has the nickname 'Granny'.) I'm quoting this from a press release – from the *Herald* itself – accessed readily via the Internet. The same press release states: 'The Herald has reinforced its position as a newspaper that makes a difference.' Oneroa Stewart was not so easy to track down. Having completed his studies, he currently lives in the small Northland town of Kerikeri. He also wants to make a difference.

Dr Stewart's initial response to my email contact was: 'Kia ora ra e Terry. Gee, someone out there actually reads my work! Thanks for your making contact' (Stewart 2003). According to his account, the *Herald* sourced the quotation in its editorial from an earlier news story in a regional newspaper – the *Northern News.* 'Since INL [the owners of the *Herald*] owns just about every sausage wrapper in the country I guess that's how the *Herald* got hold of the news' (ibid.). Stewart learned of the editorial *after* it was published. Was he happy with its use of his work?

> No, not really . . . I feel the *Herald* editor took some licence from my modus operandi. What I don't like to do is bash my parents (blame the victims, etc). So I certainly did not like the paragraph beginning: 'The fact is that most Māori parents in Northland put little value on education and inculcate their children similarly.' I know definitely, that when given the opportunity, parents are very keen to participate. So I designed new situations where parents could act their *tino rangatiratanga* by facilitating groups of parents to come into classes to make student compositions in *te reo* [the Māori language]. My thesis was all about following the rules of engagement between these participating parents and teachers. (ibid.)

Summarizing his research findings, Stewart writes that the Māori parent community 'Have high aspirations for the future of their children, are highly intelligent in their grammatical knowledge of *te reo*, but are often excluded by school practices, so are highly critical and often despondent at the value of schooling.' He found that pupils whose parents came into their classrooms to share in marking and assessment achieved 100 per cent in their examinations (Stewart 1997, 2003).

What is clear here is that the argument for causality in the editorial is at odds with the case Stewart has made in his thesis. The editorial writer positions readers to adopt a 'deficit' model to explain Māori non-achievement which the researcher explicitly rejects (Stewart 2003). In contrast, Stewart explains Māori non-achievement in terms of a communicative failure on the part of schools. The

Herald writer's intertextual practice has worked to hijack Stewart's research in order to bolster his/her authority while at the same time effectively (if not literally) misrepresenting his findings.

In terms of intertextual chains of distribution, it is interesting to read Stewart's comment that he was comfortable with the original *Northern News* story because he knew the local editors and could 'make well prepared statements in order to get my message across' (Stewart 2003). In other words, at the initial level of textual transformation – from thesis to news story – Stewart felt a degree of control over modes of representation. By the time this local news story had been transformed into an editorial in a large circulation daily newspaper, his control had evaporated.

A further point in respect of interdiscursivity can be made here pertaining to the accountability constraints operating on the two writers – the editorial writer and the researcher. Who or what is the editorial writer answerable to and how does this affect 'what can be said'? A *who* answer might point to a newspaper's readership profile and its ideological orientation, or to the newspaper's owner (despite assurances of editorial 'independence'). A *what* answer might be couched in terms of discourses or ideologies that legitimate the dominance of particular groups, e.g. New Zealand pakeha (van Dijk 1991: 39). As a *Māori* researcher, Stewart is constrained by culturally constructed protocols (or kawa). Regardless of any sympathy he might have for the editorial writer, 'I would not say so in public. On my own *marae* [tribally based meeting place] I am not afraid to shoot from the hip and say what has to be said to my own people. My *kaumatua* [elders] encourage and support me in this. But we prefer to hang out our own washing on our own lines and not anyone else's' (Stewart 2003). In the shift from first person singular to plural in this email message, the communal discourse of the tribe asserts itself over the individual voice of the academic researcher.

Finally, there is the question of the 'effect' of a text on individual readers. This chapter has previously identified through an interpretive act a preferred reading of a single newspaper editorial. What impact did this editorial have on the newspaper's readers? The blunt answer is that I don't know. A reasonable hypothesis would suggest that collectively, a massive diet of powerful texts framed by similar discourses are likely to play a major role in the reproduction of a particular hegemony. Readers interested in how research might be conducted on the way in which such texts have an impact at the micro-level on individual readers are referred to van Dijk's (1991) study of racism in the British press in the late 1980s.

6

Analysing Oral Texts

In this chapter, the analytical focus shifts from print texts to oral texts, in particular, conversations. Clearly, critically analysing the discourse of the latter poses particular challenges, including the need to recognize *prosodic features* (variations in pitch, loudness, tempo, emphasis and rhythm), *paralinguistic features* (such as pauses, gaps and restarts, and vocal effects such as 'tough guy' or 'baby' talk, giggling and laughing) and *kinesic signals* (body movements such as hand movements, nods of the head, facial expressions and shifts in gaze).

A pertinent challenge, however, and my starting point here, relates to the question of consumption, as in the question I asked towards the end of the last chapter: 'What impact did this editorial have on the newspaper's readers?' Such a question, if not easy to answer, is readily understood in the context of a stable, clearly bounded print text such as an editorial. How is the concept of consumption to be thought of in relation to a conversation? To address this question, I revisit a term that has been used regularly in this book: *position.*

Positioning theory and conversation

As a preamble to positioning theory, let me recall two theorists already mentioned in this book, Bakhtin and Althusser. In Chapter 2, I noted that Bakhtin was keenly interested in the ways in which individual utterances existed in a *dialogic* relationship with preceding and future utterances in what he called a chain, using the term *addressivity* to refer to that quality of an utterance which anticipates the future response of a reader or listener (Bakhtin 1986).

This view of the utterance is pertinent to conversation analysis (though you will recall that Bakhtin did not confine the term to oral texts). It is but a small step to connect Bakhtin's idea of the chain of utterances and such terms as *intertextuality* and *interdiscursivity*. However, I would argue that these terms put the focus on the relationship between texts or utterances as discursively constructed. In contrast, terms like *addressivity* put the focus on the maker of the utterance – individual subjects and the part they play in a chain. Putting it another way, the focus is on the utterer as *agent*.

In his essay, 'Ideology and ideological state apparatuses' (1971), Althusser imagines a little piece of commonplace street theatre where an individual is addressed or 'hailed' by a policeman: 'Hey, you there!' For Althusser, the focus here is not so much on individuals as on the operations of ideology. For him, 'ideology "acts" or "functions" in such a way that it "recruits" subjects among the individuals ... or "transforms" the individuals into subjects ... by that very precise operation which I have called *interpellation*' (pp. 161–3). (Elsewhere in this book, where I have referred to individuals as *subscribing* to a discourse or being *inscribed* by a discourse, I am using concepts similar to 'recruitment' and 'transformation' in the Althusserian sense.) For Althusser, the act of recognizing that one is being addressed in this act of hailing or interpellation is sufficient to turn one into a *subject* and that this subjectivization (if I might use this ugly word) is at heart ideological.

These central ideas from Bakhtin and Althusser –

dialogism, agency and subject formation via ideology or discourse – are a useful way in to positioning theory; and the latter, as I hope to show, is a useful way of approaching the critical analysis of conversational discourse.

For positioning theorists, van Langenhove and Harré (1999), conversations, viewed as a 'close-order symbolic exchange', are 'the most basic substance of the social realm' and it is in conversation that the social world is constituted via *positioning* and *rhetorical redescription* (p. 15). The latter refers to the discursive construction of versions of reality as discussed elsewhere in this book. *Positioning* is a fluid process, which van Langenhove and Harré describe as 'the discursive construction of personal stories that make a person's actions intelligible and relatively determinate as social acts and within which the members of a conversation have specific locations' (ibid.: 16). Any act of positioning tends to provisionally assign 'roles' to members of an exchange, and these roles help constitute the stories that make members' actions meaningful. In conversation, one can both position oneself *and* be positioned – as powerful or powerless, authoritative or lacking in authority, dependent or independent, and so on (ibid.: 17).

Positioning theory's emphasis on the concept of speech-act draws attention to the *illocutionary force* of an utterance, that is, what is achieved in the act itself, for example, obtaining agreement or issuing a command. Positioning theorists view the structure of conversations as tri-polar – as consisting of 'positions, storylines and relatively determinate speech-acts'. Analysis, then, aims to uncover ways in which particular speech-acts serve to position members of a conversation and in turn how these positions work to constitute various storylines. The word 'relatively' draws attention to the fluid nature of the process and ways in which shifts in position can lead to changes in storyline.

Analysing a sample text

It needs emphasizing that there is no one, authorized way of undertaking a critical conversation analysis. (Readers are referred to Pomerantz and Fehr (1997) and ten Have (1999) for a more detailed introduction to the subject than can be provided here.) My approach draws on Fairclough (1992a) and Gee (1996) as well as the positioning theorists discussed above.

Box 6.1 is a transcription of part of an interview between a teacher/interviewer and a Year 4 New Zealand pupil. The interview data comes from the National Education Monitoring Project (NEMP), which has the ongoing task of assessing and reporting on the achievement of New Zealand school pupils in all curriculum areas at two class levels, Year 4 and Year 8. The child in this interview is describing, interpreting and responding to a painting, which is reproduced in Figure 6.1 (Flockton and Crooks 2000).

Box 6.1   Transcript of assessment interview

[Interviewer is abbreviated to '**I**' and child to '**C**']

(General setting: Interviewer and child are sitting side by side at wooden desks. The video camera is positioned to film their exchange from front on.)

Interviewer's indication of intention

Stanza 1

1.   **I.**   I'm going to show you some reproductions or copies of two paintings made by New Zealand artists. *(Gives child laminated copy of the painting. From time to time throughout the interview the child*

bends the painting towards himself to view it more closely.)

2.   **C.**   OK. *[fall/rise intonation]*

Child's description of the first painting

Stanza 2

3.   **I.**   I'd like you to describe <u>exactly</u> what you see in this picture...

4.   **C.**   *(leans over painting looking at it intently, then straightens up)* .... umm

5.   **I.**   Imagine I've never seen it before and you're explaining it to me.

6.   **I.**   Describe <u>exactly</u> what is in the picture.

7.   **C.**   Well it's a picture of ... ahh ... um ... a boy with a machine, with a toy machine gun

8.   **C.**   and a grand ... well it seems like Christmas or happy birthdays or something so the grandpa's giving them ... um ..... a machine gun.

9.   **C.**   And another present for the other boy ... other boy *(looks towards interviewer).*

10.   **I.**   Oh, so one for both of them?

11.   **C.**   Yeah.

Child's thought/s in response to the painting

Stanza 3

12.   **I.**   Can you tell me what the picture makes you think about Joshua?

13.   **C.**   Toys *[falling intonation]*

14.   **I.**   Ah hum.

Child's feeling/s in response to the painting

Stanza 4

15.	I.	How does the painting make you feel?
16.	C.	*(scratches head, then brings closed hand to rest against right cheek, purses lips.)* .... kind of happy *[fall/rise intonation]*
17.	C.	... makes me feel just a little bit, you know, sort of sad *[falling intonation]* as well
18.	C.	by the way the grandpa's looking.
19.	I.	All right, so which part makes you happy?
20.	C.	Well, the boy getting that, I suppose.
21.	I.	The boy getting toys...
22.	I.	... and a bit sad about? What's he looking like that's making you feel a little bit sad?
23.	C.	..... Well, he just seems all hunched up
24.	C.	as if he's, you know, giving all ... um ... his lifetime, lifetime possessions or something to the to the wee boys,
25.	C.	as if he's going to die soon or something...
26.	C.	I don't know *[fall/rise intonation]*.
27.	I.	Yeah, I suppose that's a possibility.
28.	I.	So he might be dying soon so he's giving all his lifetime possessions away?
29.	C.	Yeah.

Child's explanation for a painter's method of execution

Stanza 5

30.	I.	Why do you think the artist did the painting this particular way?
31.	C.	*(cocks head to his left, then straightens up, purses lips)* .... Well *[fall/rise intonation]*, I s'pose to just show how...
32.	C.	Ohh, push out his feelings I s'pose.

33.	**I.**	Push out his feelings?
34.	**C.**	Express his feelings in his work.
35.	**I.**	Yeah.

Child's interpretation of the painting

Stanza 6.

36.	**I.**	And what do you think he's trying to say to you,
37.	**I.**	in the picture,
38.	**I.**	or to us?
39.	**C.**	*(looks straight ahead)* ..... umm .... play with a present,
40.	**C.**	or enjoy your present or
41.	**C.**	.... umm ..... give presents too.
42.	**I.**	All right.

It needs emphasizing that the transcription itself is already an act of interpretation. In the first instance, Box 6.1 is the product of a close viewing of a NEMP videotape by two researchers, thus enhancing its reliability as a record. However, as a record it is still selective and interpretive. It is selective, for example, in its choice of salient prosodic features and kinesic signals. It is interpretive in its division into lines and stanzas (discussed below) and in its choice of such words as 'intently' (line 4).

Moreover, the transcript is constructed in accordance with a set of conventions. Box 6.1 uses Gee's (1996) procedure of dividing oral text into stanzas and lines.

> Lines are usually clauses (simple sentences); stanzas are sets of lines about a single minimal topic, organized rhythmically and syntactically so as to hang together in a particularly tight way. The stanza takes a particular perspective on a character, action, even, claim, or piece of information. (p. 94)

Figure 6.1 Michael Smither. *Gifts*

Stanza 2, for example, is concerned with the child's attempt at describing the painting. It is a courtesy to readers to specify the conventions which underpin a particular transcript. Conventions related to Box 6.1 are:

- Stanzas and lines are used to structure the transcript.
- Kinesic signals are italicized inside round brackets.
- Prosodic and paralinguistic features (such as intonation) are italicized inside square brackets.
- Stressed words are underlined.
- Kinesic, prosodic and paralinguistic features are selectively rather than exhaustively identified.

81

- The overlapping of speakers, where selected, are described in round brackets and italicized.
- Voiced hesitations (e.g. ah, um) are marked.
- Pauses are marked with dots (. . .) with the number of dots indicating an estimated length of pause.

The analysis that follows is illustrative rather than exhaustive, and utilizes Fairclough's (1992a) nine properties discussed in Chapter 4.

1 Interactional control

This property is particularly pertinent to conversations and is concerned with such aspects as turn-taking, topic selection, control of the agenda and questions of who initiates and terminates interactions. Box 6.1. is clearly highly controlled. The interviewer follows almost exactly a predetermined sequence of questioning cues developed by the NEMP assessment task development panel for Art (Flockton and Crooks 2000: 38). She initiates and terminates the conversation and introduces the topics around which each stanza is focused. There is a clear power imbalance. In terms of positioning theory, the interviewer might be viewed as having been assigned the role of 'interested party', which reduces the sense that she is a tester. The child might be though of as having been assigned the role of 'art critic'. However, as we shall see, while this division might *appear* to construct a story where the child is a powerful source of knowledge, there is another story being told which defines and constrains the way the child can *act as critic*.

2 Modality

Modality refers to the strength with which a particular proposition or statement is endorsed. Typically, modality is shown through the use of modal auxiliaries (e.g. 'may') and tempering adverbs (e.g. 'possibly'). In Box 6.1 the child is often tentative and exploratory in making statements. This is shown by the use of the verb 'seems' (lines 8 and 23), the verb 'suppose' (lines 20, 31 and 32), and the adverbial phrases 'kind of' (line 16), 'a little bit' and 'sort of' (line 17). This tentativeness is reinforced by prosodic features such as pauses (such as the one in line 16) and fall/rise intonation patterns (e.g. lines 16 and 26), and the kinesic signal in line 16. In general, the child might be described as resisting any invitation to be definitive in his response to the painting.

3 Politeness

This property relates to the property of force, which is in turn concerned with the nature of particular speech acts. This property is of particular interest to positioning theory. Each of the five stanzas in Box 6.1 is initiated by the interviewer. Stanza 2 (line 3) is initiated by a sentence in the *form* of a statement containing the politely modal verb 'would like'. However, the illocutionary force of this utterance is the issuing of a command. (The command is strengthened by the modal adverb 'exactly' which is stressed and repeated.) The kinesic signal the child sends out and the voiced pause in line 4 are a clear indication of his willingness to comply with the command, to accept the position of 'expert observer'.

4 Ethos

This property of Fairclough's relates to the sorts of identity participants project through their verbal and non-verbal conduct. This interview is a formal interview situation – an examination of sorts. However, it can be argued that *one* purpose of the location of the desks relative each other is to literally put interviewer and child 'on the same side' and thereby mitigate the sense of this being an examination.

5 Connectives and argumentation

This property relates to cohesion, that is, the way in which clauses in a text relate to one another. A full analysis of cohesive devices is potentially a huge task, so I will confine myself to two patterns in respect of Box 6.1. The first of these is illustrated in stanza 2, line 10, where the pronoun 'one' is a reference to 'present' (line 9) and 'both of' is a substitution for 'a boy' (line 7) and 'other boy' (line 9). It is further illustrated in examples of lexical cohesion in such repetitions as 'happy' (line 19 referring to line 16) and 'sad' (line 22 referring to line 17). These examples of cohesion (and others) are part of a pattern where the interviewer deliberately takes up verbal cues from the child and feeds them back to him. Such feedback can be thought of as affirming speech acts, positioning the child to think of himself as someone with something worthwhile to say and whom the interviewer is keen to listen to.

The second pattern relates to the use of conjunctions in stanza 4. In lines 24 and 25 the child uses the conjunction 'as if' to link two successive subordinate adverbial clauses to the main clause 'he seems all hunched up'. In Halliday's (1994) terms, these subordinate clauses function to *enhance* the main clause. 'As if' is a conjunction of manner, suggesting a relationship of similarity or analogy. (The old man is hunched up *like* someone who is giving his lifetime possessions away.) When the interviewer responds to the child, she uses the conjunction 'so' twice without specifying the main clause. (It could be the child's observation 'he just seems all hunched up'). The functional relationship is still one of enhancement, but in this case the conjunction suggests *causality* rather than comparison. We have already noted the tentativeness suggested by the child's modal indicators. In stanza 4 the child constructs a storyline about his response to the painting that is tentative, exploratory and based on analogy. The interviewer alters this storyline by strengthening the modality and substituting an interpretation based on simple causality.

6 Transitivity and theme

As with connectives and argumentation, analysis of transitivity can be exhaustively detailed. Here, I choose to focus on the verb 'make' in stanzas 3 and 4. A study of transitivity reveals the types of processes that are coded in the structure of clauses, and how different processes can be seen to construct different storylines (as in the example of passive voice I discussed at the start of Chapter 4). The verb make/s/ing occurs in lines 12, 15, 17, 19 and 22, mostly used by the interviewer in questions which powerfully frame the terms in which the child can couch his response to the painting. Each of these instances occurs in the pattern subject–verb–object–infinitive – a transitive pattern – which (in terms of Fairlough's process categories discussed in Chapter 4) suggests an *action* process where an agent (in this case the painting) acts upon a goal (in this case the subject viewing the painting). What this analysis suggests is that the child is being powerfully positioned by the interviewer to accept a storyline about how to read artworks. In this storyline, the artwork is constructed as *causing* an interpretation to happen in the viewing subject. The insistent repetition of the verb make and the pattern of transitivity allow the child little option than to buy into this storyline.

7 and 8 Word meaning and wording

As discussed in Chapter 4, both of these relate to vocabulary. In the child's responses in stanza 2, the vocabulary tends to be concrete ('toy machine gun' and the evocation of specific social occasions). The child is positioned to respond in this way by at least two things the interviewer does. First, the interviewer demands an exact description. Second, he is asked to describe what is *in* the picture, not the picture itself. The insertion of the preposition constructs a storyline of the painting as *containing* a scene which it in some way represents. In the child's responses in stanza 4, the vocabulary tends to be abstract ('happy', 'sad'). Again, the child is positioned to resort to abstract language by the interviewer's use of the word 'feel'.

9 Metaphor

Metaphor is also related to vocabulary. The example I will discuss occurs in stanza 6, in the interviewer's question (going along with the child's identification of the artist as male), 'what do you think he's trying to say to you' (line 36). 'Say' is a personification, since paintings don't talk. Again, the child is being positioned to accept a storyline about an artwork as having a message, which its maker intends to communicate to a viewer. The child accepts this storyline and responds with three messages couched in the form of three somewhat morally tinged injunctions which are in marked contrast to the complex exploration he has begun in stanza 4.

This foregoing discussion hardly constitutes the last word that can be said about this exchange. However, on the basis of this analysis, I would provisionally conclude that this is a highly controlled interaction where the child is invited to take on the identity of art critic, but where the terms in which the child can exercise this 'role' are largely predetermined. The child's exploration of the painting's meaning is clearly exploratory and tentative and somewhat at odds with the interviewer's demand for more certainty. The interviewer makes extensive use of feedback, thus affirming the child's responses. However, at crucial junctures, this feedback subtly changes the nature of the process embedded in the child's description of the painting's content. Moreover, throughout the interview, the child is powerfully positioned to accept a particular storyline about how viewers make meaning in response to artworks.

Focusing on sociocultural and discourse practice

The immediate situation of this text is an assessment task conducted in 1999 by an experienced teacher with one of 1440 Year 4 children representing about 2.5 per cent of all children at this level in New Zealand schools (Flockton and Crooks 2000). The videoed interview is a tiny item of data in a large-scale educational monitoring project aimed at providing 'information on how well overall national standards are being maintained and where improvements might be needed' (p. 4). The National Education Monitoring Project (NEMP) is comparable with similar projects in other settings, is regularly reviewed by international scholars and is highly regarded in New Zealand and elsewhere.

The task itself was developed by a curriculum advisory panel appointed by NEMP. A comparison of the transcript and the task instructions show how closely the interviewing teacher adhered to the latter (Flockton and Crooks 2000: 38). As a discourse practice, this interview is a clear instance of manifest intertextuality. In this case, a written text as developed by a curriculum panel, is overtly drawn on in the production of an oral text – the actual interview (and many others like it). As a genre, we might include it in the category 'structured interview' and compare it with other examples where interviewers follow a pre-determined line of questioning.

Of key interest are issues of interdiscursivity. The focus of this assessment task is the ability of students to 'describe and interpret imagery and art making inform-ation in observed pictures, and express a personal response' (ibid.: 38). As this book has been emphasizing, however, processes such as describing, interpreting and responding are not neutral, but are constructed in dis-course. As the analysis has shown, this transcript (and the task it is based on) constructs description, interpretation and response in particular ways that subscribe to parti-cular discourses available in educational contexts and in society at large. In doing so, other ways in which description, interpretation and response can be con-structed are marginalized.

In respect of issues of distribution and consumption, we know that the video upon which this transcript was based was made available to a marker – an experienced teacher who would have scored the child's responses in accordance with their own professional judgement gui-ded by a formal marking rubric. Once marked, the video was added to NEMP's impressive store of assessment data. However, what *will* have been widely distributed is the task itself in a number of textual settings – the publication quoted in this chapter, as a stand-alone assessment exemplar, in various professional development settings, and so on. One can only speculate on its 'effect', but it would not be unreasonable to suggest that it would have been a powerful instrument in providing primary tea-chers with a 'language' with which to *word* response to art.

The analysis featured in this chapter is not taken from an actual project. Such a project would require far more textual samples for its corpus and far more respondents. However, it does point to the usefulness of CDA for revealing the discursive substratum beneath the relatively opaque surface of texts. The aim is not to reveal some sinister and manipulative hand aiming to impose power over others, but to provide opportunities for critical detachment and review of the ways in which discourses act to pervade and construct our textual and social practices in a range of contexts.

References

Althusser, L. (1971) 'Ideology and ideological state apparatuses (Notes towards an investigation)', in L. Althusser (ed.), *Lenin and Philosophy and Other Essays* (trans. B. Brewster). London: NLB, pp. 121–73.

Andrews, R. (ed.) (1992) *Rebirth of Rhetoric: Essays in Language, Culture and Education*. London: Routledge.

Bakhtin, M. (1986) 'The problem with speech genres', in C. Emerson and M. Holquist (eds), *Speech Genres and Other Late Essays: M. M. Bakhtin* (trans. V. McGee). Austin: University of Texas Press, pp. 60–102.

Cope, B. and Kalantzis, M. (eds) (1993) *The Powers of Literacy: A Genre Approach to Teaching Writing*. Pittsburgh: University of Pittsburgh Press.

Dale, R. (1989) *The State and Education Policy*. Milton Keynes: Open University Press.

Damasio, A. (1999) *The Feeling of What Happens: Body, Emotion and the Making of Consciousness*. London: Vintage.

Denzin, N. and Lincoln, Y. (eds) (1994) *Handbook of Qualitative Research*. Thousand Oaks, CA: Sage Publications, Inc, pp. 138–57.

Derewianka, B. (1998) *A Grammar Companion for Primary Teachers*. Newtown, NSW: PETA.

Fairclough, N. (1992a) *Discourse and Social Change*. Cambridge: Polity Press.

Fairclough, N. (ed.) (1992b) *Critical Language Awareness*. London: Longman.

Fairclough, N. (1995) *Critical Discourse Analysis.* London: Longman.

Fairclough, N. and Wodak, R. (1997) 'Critical discourse analysis', in T. van Dijk (ed.), *Discourse as Social Interaction: Discourse Studies: A Multidisciplinary Introduction Volume 1.* London: Sage, pp. 258–84.

Flockton, L. and Crooks, T. (2000) *Art Assessment Results 1999.* Dunedin, NZ: Educational Assessment Research Unit.

Foucault, M. (1980) 'Truth and power', in M. Foucault, *Power/Knowledge: Selected Interviews and Other Writings 1972–1977* (ed. C. Gordon). New York: Pantheon Books, pp. 109–33.

Foucault, M. (1991) 'Politics and the study of discourse', in G. Burchell, C. Gordon and P. Miller (eds), *The Foucault Effect: Studies in Governmentality.* London: Harvester Wheatsheaf, pp. 53–72.

Freedman, A. and Medway, P. (1994) 'Introduction: new views of genre and their implications for education', in A. Freedman and P. Medway (eds), *Teaching and Learning Genre.* Portsmouth, NH: Boynton/Cook, pp. 1–24.

Gee, J. (1996) *Social Linguistics and Literacies: Ideology in Discourses* (second edn). London: Taylor & Francis Ltd.

Halliday, M. (1994) *An Introduction to Functional Grammar* (2nd edn). London: Edward Arnold.

Halliday, M. and Hasan, R. (1985) *Language, Context, and Text: Aspects of Language in a Social-Semiotic Perspective.* Geelong, Victoria: Deakin University.

Hodge, R. and Kress, G. (1988) *Social Semiotics.* Cambridge: Polity Press.

Janks, H. (1994) 'Developing Critical Language Awareness materials for a post-apartheid South Africa', *English in Aotearoa,* 22, 46–55.

Janks, H. (1997) 'Critical discourse analysis as a research tool', *Discourse: Studies in the Cultural Politics of Education,* 18 (3), 329–42.

Janks, H. and Ivanic, R. (1992) 'CLA and emancipatory discourse', in N. Fairclough (ed.), *Critical Language Awareness*. London: Longman, pp. 305–31.

Kincheloe, J. and McLaren, P. (1994) 'Rethinking critical theory and qualitative research', in N. Denzin and Y. Lincoln (eds), *Handbook of Qualitative Research*. Thousand Oaks, CA: Sage, pp. 138–57.

Kress, G. (1993) 'Genre as social process', in B. Cope and M. Kalantzis (eds), *The Powers of Literacy: A Genre Approach to Teaching Writing*. Pittsburgh: University of Pittsburgh Press, pp. 22–37.

Lankshear, C. (1994) *Critical Literacy*. Belconnen, ACT: Australian Curriculum Studies Association.

Locke, T. (2001) 'Questions of professionalism: erosion and reclamation', *CHANGE: Transformations in Education*, 4 (2), 30–40.

McLaughlin, T. (1995) 'Introduction', in F. Lentricchia and T. McLaughlin (eds), *Critical Terms for Literary Study* (2nd edn). Chicago: University of Chicago Press, pp. 1–8.

Morgan, W. (1992) *A Post-Structuralist English Classroom: The Example of Ned Kelly*. Melbourne: Victorian Association for the Teaching of English.

Morgan, W. (1997) *Critical Literacy in the Classroom: The Art of the Possible*. London: Routledge.

Paltridge, B. (2000) *Making Sense of Discourse Analysis*. Gold Coast: Antipodean Educational Enterprises.

Parker, I. and The Bolton Discourse Network (1999) *Critical Textwork: An Introduction to Varieties of Discourse and Analysis*. Milton Keynes: Open University Press.

Patterson, A. (1997) 'Critical discourse analysis: a condition of doubt', *Discourse: Studies in the Cultural Politics of Education*, 18 (3), 425–35.

Pennycook, A. (2001) *Critical Applied Linguistics: A Critical Introduction*. Mahwah, NJ: Lawrence Erlbaum Associates.

Pomerantz, A. and Fehr, B. (1997) 'Conversation analysis: an approach to the study of social action as sense making practices', in T. van Dijk (ed.), *Discourse as Social Interaction. Discourse Studies: A Multidisciplinary Introduction Volume 2*. London: Sage, pp. 64–91.

Pinker, S. (1994) *The Language Instinct: The New Science of Language and Mind*. London: Penguin.

Pinker, S. (1997) *How the Mind Works*. London: Penguin.

Stewart, A. (1997) *The Role of the Māori Parent Community in the Delivery of the Te Rea Maori Curriculum*. Unpublished EdD thesis, University of Auckland, Auckland.

Stewart, A. (agstew@clear.net.nz) (September–October 2003) Various emails to T. Locke (t.locke @waikato.ac.nz) on the subject of Stewart's doctoral thesis and its use by the *New Zealand Herald*.

Te Puni Kokiri (1999) *Māori Unemployment*. Retrieved 30 October, 2003 from http://www.tpk.govt.nz/maori/work/fs3unemploy.pdf.

ten Have, P. (1999) *Doing Conversation Analysis: A Practical Guide*. London: Sage.

van Dijk, T. (1991) *Racism and the Press*. London: Routledge.

van Dijk, T. (1993) 'Principles of critical discourse analysis', *Discourse and Society*, 4 (2), 249–83.

van Langenhove, L. and Harré, R. (1999) 'Introducing positioning theory', in R. Harré and L. van Langenhove (eds), *Positioning Theory: Moral Contexts of Intentional Action*. Maldon: Blackwell, pp. 14–31.

Wallace, C. (1992) 'Critical literacy awareness in the EFL classroom', in N. Fairclough (ed.), *Critical Language Awareness*. London: Longman, pp. 59–92.

Wodak, R. (1996) *Disorders of Discourse*. London: Longman.

Wodak, R. (2001) 'What CDA is about – a summary of its history, important concepts and its developments', in R. Wodak and M. Meyer (eds), *Methods of Critical Discourse Analysis*. London: Sage, pp. 1–13.

Index